By the Word of Their Testimony

"And they overcame him because of the
blood of the Lamb and because of the
word of their testimony…"
Revelation 12:11

Enter His Gates with Thanksgiving
and His Courts with Praise

Book 11

Erin Thiele

Cover Design by Tara Thiele • NarrowRoad Publishing House

D0862635

By the Word of Their Testimony

Enter His Gates with Thanksgiving and His Courts with Praise

By Erin Thiele

Published by:
NarrowRoad Publishing House
POB 830
Ozark, MO 65721 U.S.A.

The materials from Restore Ministries were written for the sole purpose of encouraging women. For more information, please take a moment to visit us at: **EncouragingWomen.org** or **RestsoreMinistries.net**.

Unless otherwise indicated, most Scripture verses are taken from the *New American Standard Bible* (NASB). Scripture quotations marked KJV are taken from the *King James Version* of the Bible, and Scripture quotations marked NIV are taken from the *New International Version*. Our ministry is not partial to any particular version of the Bible but **loves** them all so that we are able to help every woman in any denomination who needs encouragement and who has a desire to gain greater intimacy with her Savior.

ISBN: 1-931800-94-4
ISBN 13: 978-1-931800-94-5

Contents

Introduction

Your Divine Appointment

"I was **crying** to the LORD with my voice,
And He **answered me** from His holy mountain"
—Psalm 3:4

Have you been searching for marriage help? It's not by chance, nor is it by coincidence, that you are reading this book. God has heard your cry for help in your marriage dilemma. He predestined this DIVINE APPOINTMENT to give you the hope that you so desperately need right now!

If you have been told that your marriage is hopeless or that without your spouse's help your marriage cannot be restored then this is the book you need. Read this over and over so you will begin to believe that God is MORE than able to restore ANY marriage, including YOURS!

We know and understand what you are going through since WE, and MANY others who have come to our ministry for help, have a restored marriage and family! No matter what others have told you, your marriage is NOT hopeless We KNOW, after twenty five years of ministry, that God is able to restore ANY marriage, even YOURS!

If you have been crying out to God for more help, someone who understands, then join our Internet Restoration Fellowship to help you see your marriage through to restoration during your rebuilding phase of your journey Since beginning this fellowship, we have seen more marriages restored on a regular basis than we ever thought possible!

So, if you are really serious in your desire to restore your marriage, then our fellowship is the answer. For more information or to join, go to our website RMIEW.com. We would love for you to be a part of our Restoration Fellowship!

Who are we and what are we hoping to do?

Restore Ministries helps those who have found themselves in a hopeless situation: couples whose spouse is in adultery, has left, has filed for divorce, or any other seemingly impossible marital situation. These broken people have often sought help, but everyone (many times even their pastors) have told them their marriage was hopeless. However, we not only believe that no marriage is hopeless – regardless of the circumstances—we know they aren't. That's why we offer hope, help and encouragement through our website, our Restoration Fellowship, and a variety of resources including a variety of newsletters to spiritual feed and uplift you daily!

In 2001, Restoration Fellowship was birthed to minister more effectively to the needs of those seriously seeking restoration. Within a year the fellowship grew to over 400 committed members and increases daily with members from all over the world.

Restore Ministries has never sought advertising or paid for placement in search engines but has instead grown by word of mouth. We also take no support from anyone but the individuals themselves who are seeking restoration so that we are never told we must comprise sharing His full truths. Though often ostracized by the established church, because of those who have cried out to God for help when their own church, pastor family and friends who offered them no hope or support, we have given them hope and we have become an oasis in the desert for the desperate, the hurting, the rejected.

Often accused of being extreme, radical, out-of-balance or legalistic, the message in all our resources is founded firmly on the Word of God only, encouraging those seeking restoration to live the message that Jesus proclaimed, beginning with the familiar Beatitudes.

RMI teaches the good news of God's Word to bring healing to the brokenhearted, comfort to those in pain, and freedom to prisoners of despondency and sin through the truth of His Word, giving them the hope that is "against all hope" through the Power of Jesus Christ, the Mighty Counselor and Good Shepherd.

Our site and our resources minister to the hurting all over the world with the intent of creating a deeper and more intimate walk with the Lord that results in the hurting healed, the bound freed, the naked clothed, the lost saved and broken marriages restored We minister to women from more than 15 countries including Switzerland, Hong Kong, New Zealand, Sweden,

Philippines, Brazil and Germany, with large followings in Australia, Canada, and Africa. Our books have been translated into Spanish, Portuguese, Tagalog (Filipino), Afrikaans, and French. Also Slovakian, Chinese, Russian, Italian and some Hindi.

Jesus said that you "will know them by their fruits" that's why this book and all our *By the Word of Their Testimony* books are filled with testimonies of hopeless marriages that were restored marriages that give glory to God and to the Power of His Word Our *WOTT* books are growing at such a phenomenal rate that we were once unable to keep up with getting them published. Now we have a full team devoted to keeping up.

If you have any doubt about the validly of our ministry, you won't after reading this and our other awesome books. Each will show you not only hopeless marriages that were restored, but more importantly, it will show you men and women who have been completely transformed into God-lovers and are now committed on-fire Christians, many of whom were saved through this ministry.

Below is a small sampling of the letters of gratitude that Restore Ministries has received. Please note when you read the letters that they give all the praise and glory to the Lord. This ministry was founded and continues to grow on the premise that "if He be lifted up, He will draw all men to Himself" and "the Lord will share His glory with no man."

"Let Another Praise You" Proverbs 27:2

"Thank you, Thank you, Thank you for allowing God to use you, thank you to all the team members of RMI continue to do the work of God. Thank you especially to Erin for her lovely encouragement and support, thanks for making your resources available for free I could not afford it with tears in my eyes you guys will have no idea the way that you have blessed my life. Thank you for your courses, resources, books, encouragements and testimonies. I love you all so much."

~ *From Kimberley in Jamaica*

I want to thank you for giving me hope. For giving me a roadmap to restore my family. For changing my life. I have seen my life transformed since I found this course a month and 9 days ago.

The testimonies in the book By the Word of Their Testimony encouraged me to keep going. Each testimony had one thing I could relate to. I learned so much from them. One had my almost same exact story. They were amazing!

~ From Aracely in California

From the testimonies that I have read [By The Word of Their Testimony], I have realized the great depth that women have come to have and that it has helped them to transform their personal lives with God and with their relationships with their partners, it has surprised me how many marriages have been restored and how the Lord has blessed them.

~ From Mavis in Panama

We put this book and all our *Word of Their Testimony* books together because we believe that as you spend some time reading these incredible and awesome testimonies of seemingly hopeless marriages that were miraculously restored you will be encouraged and know without a doubt...

NOTHING IS IMPOSSIBLE WITH GOD!!

Nothing is Impossible
with God!

"Looking at them, Jesus said,
'With people it is impossible,
but not with God;
for all things are possible with God.'"
Mark 10:27

*"And they overcame him because of the blood of the Lamb and because of the **word of THEIR testimony**, and they did not love their life even to death." Rev. 12:11.*

The following testimonies are filled with miracles of men and women who took God at His Word and believed that "nothing was impossible with God!" Those who have had the miracle of a restored marriage have several things in common. All "delighted themselves in the Lord" and He gave them "the desires of their heart." All of them "hoped against hope" when their situation seemed hopeless.

All of them "fought the good fight" and "finished their course." All of them were determined "not to be overcome with evil" but instead to "overcome evil with good." All were willing to "bless their enemies" and to pray for them that "despitefully used and persecuted them." All "turned the other cheek" and "walked the extra mile." All realized that it was "God who removed lover and friend far from" them and it was God who "made them a loathing" to their spouse. All of them understood and believed that it is NOT the will of man (or woman) but the "will of God" who can "turn the heart" whichever way He chooses.

All refused to fight in "the flesh" but chose to battle "in the spirit." None were concerned to protect themselves, but trusted themselves "to Him who judges righteously." All of their trust was "in the Lord" because their trust was "the Lord." All released their attorneys (if that was part of their testing) since they "would rather be wronged or defrauded." All of them "got out of the way of wickedness" and "let the unbeliever leave" since they "were called to peace." All refused to do "evil for evil or insult for insult." All loved their spouse who may have been unfaithful because they knew that "love never fails."

This is the same journey that the Lord took me on back in 1989. That year I made a promise to God that if He would restore my marriage to my husband, I would devote my life to telling others about Him and His desire and ability to restore ANY marriage no matter what the circumstances. The Lord was faithful and restored my marriage, suddenly, two years later after a divorce. (Yes! AFTER a divorce!) Now I faithfully, with the Lord's continued help, love, support, and guidance, spread the GOOD news that nothing—NOT A THING—is impossible with God!

It is important to know that our ministry was FOUNDED to help all those who were told by pastors and Christian friends that their situations were HOPELESS. Those who come to us for hope are facing a spouse who is deep in adultery, who has moved out (often in with the other man or woman who committed adultery with), who has already filed for divorce or whose divorce has gone through. 99% of those who come, come alone for help since their spouse is not interested in saving their marriage, but is desperately trying to get out. Over 95% claim that they are Christians and most are married to Christians.

Over half are in some type of Christian service and many of the men who are involved with other woman are pastors who have left not only their wife and children, but their church as well.

If you, or if someone you know, is facing devastation in their marriage, there is hope. Read these awesome testimonies that prove that God is MORE than able to restore ANY marriage—even YOURS!

Chapter 1

Kristen

"You need not fight in this battle;
station yourselves, stand and see the salvation
of the Lord on your behalf . . ."
—2 Chronicles 20:17

"Shouting Profanity Loud Enough for Our Neighbors to Hear!"

Kristen, how did your restoration actually begin?

It all started years ago, but everything intensified a little over three years ago. Several things happened in our lives, many blessings, but with these blessings came many problems. The problems that my husband had with his family came to the forefront and he became overwhelmed.

I didn't know how a Christian wife should behave and I was pressuring him to be someone he was not. So with all the problems that came up with his family, everything became very difficult between us, and the more pressure I put on him. With the birth of our son, things only got worse. We had different opinions about how to raise him, and that's when my husband asked me to leave the house for the first time. It didn't happen right after the birth, but the day after my son turned two. And because I was very proud, when he asked me to leave—I left in a huff— with my son on my hip I slammed the door shouting profanity loud enough for our neighbors to hear!

How did God change your situation, Kristen, as you sought Him wholeheartedly?

The Lord has been working on me for some time. Today I see that this has been happening even before I got married. As the problems in my marriage intensified, the Lord made this work that He had already started more perfect. Not that He has finished with me yet, because I know my Restoration Journey with Him will never end until I meet Him face-to-face. But due to His love and patience He has improved what He had started in me. He has helped me to be more patient, more understanding and to remain quiet in situations where I would always have had an opinion. Based on what I already shared, having a gentle and quiet spirit is not what I had when I was asked to leave our home.

What principles, from God's Word (or through our resources), Kristen, did the Lord teach you during this trial?

The principles of a gentle and quiet spirit, the power and freedom from being submissive to all authority and talking only to God about everything that happens in my life. Never discussing anything with anyone but Him. These principles are not easy to follow, and I confess that I still stumble occasionally. But due only to His enormous grace and love, the Lord has helped me get back on track and trust Him to change me.

Another hugely important principle to be followed for restoration is to tithe to your storehouse. Since I've been following this one principle faithfully, I can see that's when my journey changed course and what had previously been stolen from me I began receiving showers of blessings!

What were the most difficult times that God helped you through, Kristen?

A very difficult moment was when my Earthly Husband got sick and came to stay with us at the house where I was renting. Everything turned out so great. It also seemed to go perfectly, he was with us, with me and our son. So after a few weeks recovering, he said we should come back home, back to our house. And then, suddenly everything changed. He changed, he suddenly decided he wanted to go home before he was fully recovered and when I left, he told me that we could not come back home. Then the Lord reminded me of this verse in Proverbs 21:1 "The king's heart is like channels of water in the hand of the Lord; He turns it wherever He wishes." GOD turned my Earthly Husband towards me, then GOD turned it away. So I was able to dance and praise Him. My son and I put on dance music rejoicing because we knew God would win this battle for us and it had to be getting close just as it says in 2 Chronicles 20:17 "You need not fight in this battle; station yourselves, stand and see the salvation of the Lord on your behalf...Do not fear or be dismayed...the Lord is with you."

Kristen, what was the "turning point" of your restoration?

The turning point is when I got a job near my home. This was quite unexpected, as my Earthly Husband asked me to get a job. I didn't want to, because besides having a boy of only three years old, I saw through the biblical principles that are in the book How God Can and Will Restore Your Marriage and in the book A Wise Woman, where it says that the woman should stay at home, helping her husband in the home, taking care of the home and children. Yet, He also says in His Word we are to submit to our husbands. So I spoke to my Heavenly Husband He told me to trust Him. If He didn't want me to get a job I wouldn't find one. If I did, it was His plan and His alone—not my Earthly Husband or mine trying to restore my marriage.

Tell us HOW it happened, Kristen? Did your husband just walk in the front door? Kristen, did you suspect or could you tell you were close to being restored?

When the Lord thought it was time, that I was ready for restoration, not only did I get a job in something I never imagined doing, because it needed training I didn't have. But what made it so beautiful is that I work very close to my house and can often work from home with a teenage babysitter who plays with my son while I work. Being home means I can take care of the house and utilize so much of what Erin teaches in workers@home.

Most interestingly, the Lord used it for good "Everything works together for good for those who love God and are called according to His Purpose" Romans 8:28. So, because of the times my job required me to be at work each morning, I talked to my Earthly Husband and explained that for me to accept, I'd need to stay at our house. I'd used this as the fleece, just lay it out before the Lord. I thought for sure he would not agree and I'd be able to refuse the job offer. But instead he insisted that I accept and move back home—the Lord did the rest!!! So I've been home for almost two months.

As so many restoration testimonies say, I too confess that it has not been easy, because as it was said in one of the courses, I still have a newborn on my hands (my Earthly Husband). But the Lord is dealing with me first and His work will be completed. What's important is that we are home, as a family!

Would you recommend any of our resources in particular that helped you, Kristen?

Yes, I would recommend the books How God Can Restore Your Marriage, A Wise Woman, the courses (I'm still doing these despite my busy schedule). I decided to go back to the lessons, because each one has changed my way of thinking and how I feel about everything in my life. I also highly recommend the book Finding Life Abundant, which has given me a wonderful experience in finding my Heavenly Husband and without Him I would never be able to do what I'm doing now!

Would you be interested in helping encourage other women, Kristen?

Yes, I am ready to help as many women need hope.

Either way, Kristen, what kind of encouragement would you like to leave women with, in conclusion?

Don't give up on your miracle. But mostly fall in love with the Word of God and the Lord as your Heavenly Husband. He is for life, and the more of Him, the more blessings He will add to you!

Chapter 2

Olivia

"Then I will make up to you for the years
That the swarming locust has eaten."
—Joel 2:25

"Restored in the Middle of the Worldwide Covid-19 Pandemic!"

Olivia, how did your restoration actually begin?

It all started 4+ years ago, my husband and I had just celebrated our 11-year wedding anniversary. About two weeks later, I started to notice that my husband was acting and treating me completely different. As I looked at him, I thought, "this is not my husband, something has gotten ahold of him; it is not good and it is evil." He had turned into someone that I didn't even recognize or know. From that moment on, everything turned upside down.

He pulled away from me. He hardly talked to me. I started to seek and pray to God to find any testimonies of God restoring marriages that went through what I was going through. I did not know it at the time but this was the start of my "stand" which later turned into my journey.

About 2 months later (2 days before my birthday), my husband moved out. He told me he was going to stay with one of his buddies from work because he needed space and time away. He did not want a divorce, we just needed to separate for him to clear his head.

It was right before Mother's Day and I just straight out asked him if he was with someone else. He did not want to answer. I asked again and he finally admitted that he was. It was later in the evening, he texted me that he needed to tell me something else but he was scared to tell me because he did not want to lose me. He confessed that the day he moved out he moved in with and had been living with the other woman. Later, I discovered that she was much older than us (my husband and I).

Needless to say, from then on, everything became utter hell and beyond. The things that consisted or took place were completely unbearable. I had joined the "restoration diet plan." I had lost so much weight, never wanting to eat. When I was home, I wanted to be at work. When I was at work, I wanted to be home. Thank God for my mom, who helped take care of my sons! I was literally dying. I was depressed and just had no fight in me to live.

I became part of a stander's ministry. It helped me for some time but every time things started to progress and I took a step forward, it would be soon after that I felt like I went 50 steps back. I started to feel worse about my situation versus better. I started to lose hope. I was crying more. I was becoming more discouraged and I wanted to quit (I tried many times to quit to only have my Heavenly Husband bring me back on this journey). I was just always fighting for my marriage and I was becoming exhausted. I would pray hours and hours and hours of praying scriptures with his and the OW's name in them (needless to say, many of those verses were really for me).

During this time, our home was sold out from under us (that is a whole other story and testimony) and we were forced to move into our 5th wheel trailer, where we were parked and living in a church parking lot. So, my sons and I moved into our new "home."

After a little over 2 years, my husband started to stay home more nights. Then, he was home every night. By the grace of God, they had broken up. He was home but he was not committed to me nor our marriage. He said we were just friends, best friends and I was the mother of his sons.

My husband had been home about 11 months, then all of a sudden, he started going out again. He started to work out again. Before I knew it, he was gone once more. This time, as before, news made its way back to me, that she was very, very young, more than half his age. That was a whole new level of emotions to deal with.

One night, I just cried out to God, telling Him that He needs to change this because I cannot keep living like this, something has got to change!!! I need to hear from Him in the next 24 hours in regards to my marriage or I was going to be done and believe that everything I thought I heard was from Him, was really only me telling myself I heard from God.

It was either that night or the next morning, I received a random simple response (from a complete stranger) to a prayer that I had posted for my husband, our marriage and our family on a YouTube video of a restored marriage, that changed my "stand" forever. They simply said, "hopeatlast.com is a good website to check out." Intrigued, I looked it up. I thought well, I have tried everything else, what do I have to lose, it is just 30 days. This became the start of the journey that changed my life FOREVER! What a Divine Appointment set up by my Heavenly Husband. I never looked back.

How did God change your situation, Olivia, as you sought Him wholeheartedly?

I started the courses at Hopeatlast.com. I read, How God Can and Will Restore Your Marriage, A Wise Woman and poured my heart out in the journals.I read every resource that I could from RMI. I wanted more of my Heavenly Husband. I was finally finding the hope and "thing" that was missing from my life and in my journey.

Wondering or thinking that there has to be more than this to be found, was discovered the moment I started and found this ministry. He began to change me, mold me, and transform me from the woman I had become to the woman I am now. When my husband came home the first time, I did not know that I had a restored marriage. I can also see how I was not ready to have him home yet for I was not "prepared or prepped" like I am now for his return because I was not grounded in my Heavenly Husband or His Truths.

My Heavenly Husband revealed to me in His Word and through these resources what and how a wife is supposed to be and act. What my role was and what my husband's role was. He taught me how I was to build up my husband, home and raise our sons. I was to build up my house and not tear it down like I had before. I had just as much responsibility for my marriage falling apart as my husband, I would even go as far to say, the majority, if not all of it was MY fault!

I let go of my church, which was ironic as we lived on the premises. He taught me how to tithe. I became faithful to tithe and the miracles that come from that alone changed the conditions of the way my family was living. I learned to truly surrender, let go (this was the worst for me), trust, and bring it all before Him. He became my everything. I started to have a gentle and quiet spirit and I held onto winning without a word (this was one of the hardest for me). I was different. My Beloved was all that I wanted, needed and lived for.

What principles, from God's Word (or through our resources), Olivia, did the Lord teach you during this trial?

My eyes were opened pretty wide during my journey. I learned that I was the one who tore my house down and my marriage apart. I was self-righteous, prideful, contentious, outspoken, argumentative, disrespectful, a Pharisee, and the list goes on. I shared too much with others. I talked way too much when I should have prayed, sought the Lord, then spoke. I should have backed my husband up when he would discipline our sons or be the head of our household, instead of correct him on how he did things. I knocked him down, making him smaller and smaller instead of building him up, disrespecting him and not allowing him to lead me and our children, like God made him to be and do. I opened the door, welcomed and let the enemy right in the door of my household, he did not even have to knock.

What were the most difficult times that God helped you through, Olivia?

Needless to say, with it being a 4+ year journey, I went through countless times of difficulty and the list is extremely long. I have seen and been through A LOT! But to name a few, attending our sons' activities and games alone or with him on the phone not even watching; the holidays were so tough; knowing he went on trips that I dreamed of with this OW, and with her purposely planning them on days that had significance to me so he would be gone, like my birthday or Mother's Day.

One of the hardest difficulties that just about broke me is when this OW bought my husband a wedding band and he would wear it on his wedding finger, there were a few times he had forgotten to take it off before he came over as he was trying to hide this. She also was pushing him to get a divorce. She even went as far as being willing to pay for the divorce and all that came with it. A few times he had come by to tell me he had an appointment that day and it was to meet with the divorce lawyer. He then called me to ask me what day I was off so we could go to the courthouse to sign the papers and get divorced that day (as if it happens like that). There was even a day that we had to switch vehicles and I saw the papers filled out. I kind of laughed because the papers were not even correct, he did not even fill it out right but I could tell by the nature of the writing that he was angry as he was filling it out.

Another moment was when he brought the new (other) woman to our older son's game and knowing our son said to not bring any women to his activities. He introduced her to me and our youngest son and because we did not give her the welcome he wanted, they left early and he called to cuss me out and say he was never speaking to us again.

Taking my own thoughts captive and getting out of my own head. Knowing the age of these other women was so difficult for me. Knowing he was being intimate with these other women. I struggled to let go and surrender, truly surrender so I could be set free. I doubted my Heavenly Husband would do it for me, like He had done for others because it had been taking so long.

Olivia, what was the "turning point" of your restoration?

When I started to actually let go. I struggled for years with this as I would let go but just take it right back from my Heavenly Husband because nothing was happening in my timing. I played "junior holy spirit" a lot. When I no longer desired my will to be done but His will to be done.

After coming to this ministry, I really started to apply these lessons and principles to my life. I was no longer obsessed with wanting my marriage restored. I wanted and was thirsty for my Heavenly Husband. He was starting to bless my life more than I could count or keep up with. I was starting to become free. I was light. I was enjoying my alone time with my Heavenly Husband. I was meeting my First Love for the first time and it was better than I had ever experienced before. The concerns of my husband and this OW were not the forefront of my being any longer. In fact, I started to become overly joyful saying goodbye to my husband and he was starting to get mad because I was not sulking as he left. I had a new pursuit for my heart and it was my Beloved.

I started to see my husband become dad again. He started to come home more. He started calling me more, especially when he was going on test drives for work, he would call me. He started to text me more. Whenever he got a chance, he would come home to be with us. He started to pursue me. We were becoming intimate again. We started to take family trips and go on family outings. We were beginning to become a family unit again, one that was built on the solid Rock of His Word. My Heavenly Husband was working it all out for my good, even when it felt like nothing was happening; especially because it seemed like everything was so great "over there," and it was paradise for them.

Tell us HOW it happened, Olivia? Did your husband just walk in the front door? Olivia, did you suspect or could you tell you were close to being restored?

No, he did not just walk through the door. It was actually ironic. This year on Easter weekend, my sons and I were house sitting for a family member. My husband had been there for the day but as it was nearing later in the evening, he "had" to leave. So, he said bye and left. I had not missed my husband in a long time and yet that night, it just hit me and I missed having him there at night. I cried and I did not sleep all night, I was wide awake and just talking to my Beloved.

The next morning, I realized I had forgotten something at home and I needed to pick it up. I debated on going but I felt pushed to go. As I drove up, I noticed my husband's car was here. I had this sinking feeling, hoping he didn't dare bring "her" here. I was scared, my mind wanted to run wild. I walked in; he was alone, asleep in our bed. That was it, I did not wake him, I know he knew I came by. I grabbed what I needed and left. This was my Beloved answering my prayer to show me there was trouble in paradise. A little bit later, my husband came to where we were, that was Easter day. A lot can happen in 3 days, right? From that moment on (1 month) ago, my husband has been home. My God, my God, You deserve all of the praise!!! You were faithful to fulfill what you started.

This also happened in the middle of the worldwide COVID-19 pandemic.

Did you suspect or could you tell you were close to being restored?

No, I really did not. Things seemed to have gotten worse for me. The fire was turned up big time, especially when I joined the ministry and became a part of the ministry team.

Would you recommend any of our resources in particular that helped you, Olivia?

For sure, no doubt about that. I would recommend all of the courses, Finding the Abundant Life, Poverty Mentality, How God Can and Will Restore Your Marriage, A Wise Woman, By the Word of Their Testimony, Encourager and the Devotionals.

Do you have favorite Bible verses that you would like to pass on to women reading your Testimonies? Promises that He gave you?

There are so many, but to pinpoint a few…

"Moses answered the people, 'Do not be afraid. Stand firm and you will see the deliverance the LORD will bring you today. The Egyptians you see today you will never see again. The LORD will fight for you; you need only to be still.'" Exodus 14:13-14 NIV

"But you will not even need to fight. Take your positions; then stand still and watch the LORD's victory. He is with you, O people of Judah and Jerusalem. Do not be afraid or discouraged. Go out against them tomorrow, for the LORD is with you!'" 2 Chronicles 20:17 NLT

"For this reason, I will fence her in with thornbushes. I will block her path with a wall to make her lose her way. When she runs after her lovers, she won't be able to catch them. She will search for them but not find them. Then she will think, 'I might as well return to my husband, for I was better off with him than I am now.'" Hosea 2:6-7 NLT

Would you be interested in helping encourage other women, Olivia?

ABSOLUTELY!!!! I am His vessel. I will help whomever He brings across my path. This is all for His glory, honor and praise.

Either way, Olivia, what kind of encouragement would you like to leave women with, in conclusion?

The process is tough, hard and impossible the majority of the time but He is the God of the impossible (Luke 1:37). It can be lonely and you, yourself, can be the very thing that is getting in the way of your restoration occurring. Get out of your own way. Take your thoughts captive (2 Corinthians 10:5). Press into Him. Trust Him with the process even when it does not make sense. Lean not on your own understanding (Proverbs 3:4-6).

He will restore double (Joel 2:24-25) for your trouble and make it better than it was before. He has an overflow of abundance (Ephesians 3:20) for you, your husband, your marriage and your family. He will use your testimony and use you for His glory. You only need to be still (Exodus 14:13-14).

Trust the process, even when it does not make sense or like anything is happening. One day just like I have said and so many others have said, and that someday you too will say, "this journey was worth it and I wouldn't want to change it for anything nor remove it from my life."

My Beloved, this testimony is all for Your glory, praise and honor. Thank You for turning my life upside down so that I can find and discover You. Thank You for loving me, my husband, my marriage and my family so much that You were willing to cause the insanity and chaos of how we were living to be turned upside down so we can gain and restore all that we have now and make it so much better than it was before. Thank You for making us a miracle and testimony so that we can help others and so that our family and loved ones can see that You truly are real. Miracles do happen. And Your Word NEVER returns void (Isaiah 55:11) and You are actively watching over it to perform it (Jeremiah 1:12). Hallelujah, in Your mighty and matchless name. Amen.

Chapter 3

Kiara

"The thief comes only to steal and kill
and destroy; I came that they may have
life, and have it abundantly."
—John 10:10

"I Got Involved Another Man at
My Own Wedding"

Kiara, how did your Restoration Journey actually begin?

It all started when I left the door wide open in my marriage and the enemy took over me, my life, and my marriage. It began because I was not happy the day after my huge expensive wedding. An old "friend" noticed me pouting and started up a conversation with me. At first I wanted nothing to do with him, but later in the evening after drinking way too much, he approached me asking if he could contact me after I got back from my honeymoon. It's so insane thinking about this now and I would be horrified if any of my friends told me they'd done this.

I was thirsty for praise since my fiancé (now my husband) and I fought the entire time we planned this big outrageous wedding. I wanted my dream wedding and he refused to pay for it. This guy said everything I wanted to hear, he did everything I liked and things that my husband had never done and refused to do. How foolish! I was completely blind and in the hands of the enemy who was leading me slowly off a cliff. It is so true that the enemy did come to steal, kill and destroy us.

So I got completely involved with this OM (Other Man) at my own wedding. Immediately, I started to despise, to humiliate my husband. I did everything to embarrass him. What a fool, what a horror show I had become. Every time my husband approached me to try to find out what he'd done, what we could do to mend things, I distanced myself until I asked my husband to leave. I didn't want him anymore. Dear brides I beg you never to send your husbands away. Trust me, it will end in disaster!

My husband didn't go right away, not until he was overcome by weariness and he "let me go"! He said that it was okay, he would leave the house, and that I was free. The next morning on a Sunday, I woke up to my husband packing his bags to leave the house, as we had agreed, but even though it was everything I wanted, everything I had wished for, it seemed that something inside me was happening. God already started to touch me at that moment, but the enemy was there in full force. I thought to myself, "This is really it, my husband is about to go," and then he left and my world collapsed.

How did God change your situation, Kiara, as you sought Him wholeheartedly?

As the days passed, the enemy saw that he started to lose, because I started to see my husband differently. I started to see him with different eyes. I started to be jealous of my husband who began dating right away. I told him to find someone and he did. It was easy. He was attractive and a really nice man. At the same time, the OM (Other Man) started to become uninteresting to me. Not so funny is that I started to disgust him. When I'd reach out to get together, he made excuses to not see me. Glory to God, He put a hedge of thorns around me, and I started wanting to go back to my husband, "It was better for me then than now!" I started to wish for my family, my marriage as I never felt before. I started to see how wonderful my husband was to me and to our daughter.

God took me to the desert and spoke to my heart, gave me a broken heart, filled with His Spirit. It was completely wonderful. I had not sought God in a long long time as you may have guessed. But when I was broken, I started to pray and ask Him to bring my husband back, because my family was very important to me. How wonderful God is. I began to desire it so much that I had never felt anything like it before.

It was then that my husband and I went to the same party, from our mutual friend and when my husband arrived, he was radiant, wonderful, we talked all the time and we ended up leaving the party together. We stayed together that night, but I didn't let him sleep at home (yes, another mistake). He wanted us to sleep separately, but I thought that my husband would feel like coming back faster, making it too difficult to not come home, and we stayed together in a way as we had never been.

The enemy didn't let it go and he increased the destruction due to me acting in the flesh again. After that night, it was my husband who said he didn't want me back! And that's when the huge fight started, the contentious woman was back worse than before because I just couldn't believe my husband didn't want me anymore.

What principles, from God's Word (or through our resources), Kiara, did the Lord teach you during this trial?

It was when I started to insist too much on us reconciling after my husband returned home, against his will. The fights started to happen daily, and I ended up destroying my house with my own hands. During one of the fights he decided to go sleep in his parents' house and took our daughter to sleep with him, because as it is written: It is better to live in the corner of the roof than with the quarrelsome woman in the same house.

So I went to the computer that night and researched marriage restoration and that's when I found the RMI website of this wonderful ministry!! All Honor and All Glory to You Lord for having directed me to this wonderful life saving ministry. That night I immediately started reading the book How God Can and Will Restore Your Marriage. Oh my Lord, what an incredible and wonderful book. Thank you Erin for writing this essential book for our restoration. And I really saw who I was, a quarrelsome woman, contentious, irritable, manipulative, suspicious, my daughter's boss not her mother, the spiritual leader I'd stolen from my husband. I was jealous, eavesdropped on everything. I even hired a detective to follow my husband for a month but by the grace of God I found nothing. "Blessed is the man who does not walk according to the advice of the wicked, nor stand in the way of sinners, nor sit in the circle of scoffers."

What were the most difficult times that God helped you through, Kiara?

The most difficult times were fights, as I fought in the flesh, and only afterwards did I realize that this is a spiritual battle.

Kiara, what was the "turning point" of your restoration?

Thank God I had the opportunity to read this wonderful book, I thank Erin and this ministry, and reading about my sin did not get out of my head. God showed me there at that moment what I had to do. I started seeking God with all my heart, and so I gave up my life and trusted in His word that says, "Whoever hides his sins does not prosper, but whoever confesses and abandons them finds mercy." And this is what I did, I told my husband my adultery, and he forgave me!! All Honor and all Glory to You Lord, and after only a week after I read the book my marriage was restored. I'm embarrassed to say it's only now after close to two years that I had a friend suggest submitting my testimony.

Tell us HOW it happened, Kiara? Did your husband just walk in the front door? Kiara, did you suspect or could you tell you were close to being restored?

The day I confessed to the adultery I confessed everything to my husband with many tears on both our parts. We agreed that we needed to make God first in each of our lives and first in our home. My husband began attending a church and a men's fellowship while he suggested I remain at restoration fellowship to be taught by other women.

As much as I walk in the valley of the shadows of death, I no longer fear any harm, because the Lord is with me, He is the first in my life, today I seek His face, today I have more intimacy with my HH (Heavenly Husband) and I give thanks and praise all the time, because I never ever want to go through any of this again! He wants me closer to Him, and to let go of anything that concerns me. Today what's most important is just me and Him and nobody else do I need, no other man. All I need I ask Him, I seek Him, and He comforts me, I cuddle up in His arms when I need a hug. All His love I give to my husband and daughter.

Would you recommend any of our resources in particular that helped you, Kiara?

I started course 3 the day I was restored and as of today, I have been through almost all the Abundant Life courses, all the Living Lessons and lead a Wise Woman to friends who hear about my testimony. Today I recommend and also do myself is to read the Psalm and Proverb everyday, read the Bible, I pray fast on a regular basis, and most importantly, I learned how essential it is to tithe. When I began to tithe to my storehouse, my own home became His treasured house! I must continue to give back to this wonderful ministry that feeds me spiritually.

I read the encouragement daily, I read the testimonies, I watch the encouragement videos again and again. And when I'm not feeling well, I also read the book Prison to Praise after I learned to Praise God in any and all situations. Trust God and His Word. Make your 3x5 cards, they will help you a lot. I apologize for my testimony coming so late, but it is so wonderful to talk about that which is everything to us, my husband and me. I am delighted to be able to give my testimony and I apologize for not having sent it before. Hallelujah.

Would you be interested in helping encourage other women, Kiara?

For sure! I'd love to start ministering online after having women in my home.

Either way, Kiara, what kind of encouragement would you like to leave women with, in conclusion?

May you never give up, and even after your marriages are restored! Remember, what God has united, do not separate. Don't follow in my foolishness by making your husband leave. Just know that He is working, and His plans for you are much bigger and better than yours and believe that His work will be complete, leave it to Him to do. "Like streams of water like this is the heart of the king in the hand of the Lord, who inclines him to all his will."

Seek God with all your heart, do not go back to being a fool, because with "wisdom a house is built, and with understanding it is established; and by knowledge the chambers of all precious and delightful riches will be filled." Don't ignore others who need to know the truth, help encourage other women to seek God for their marriages if they have not yet been restored. My prayer partner and I long to have a ministry in our inner city to be able to help more women, the ones who live in poverty due to lacking knowledge that I have been given. I know He will grant this desire to us at the appointed time.

Chapter 4

Lauren

"The wise woman builds her house,
But the foolish tears it down
with her own hands."
—Proverbs 14:1

"Considered Myself the 'Perfect Wife' How Ironic!"

Lauren, how did your restoration actually begin?

Hello, my name is Lauren, I am 40 years old and I have been married for almost 14 years and we have no children. I became a believer in my late teens and my husband a little before that, but once we got married we have never been very close to the Lord individually or as a couple. Over time we have become increasingly distant from anything remotely close to being a Christian. In fact, I got farther and farther away, because I was extremely proud and I always thought that I knew everything and that I could only depend on my husband, that is, God was a mere assistant to me when I needed help.

Since I completely drifted from the ways of our Lord, I always knew that I would return for the pain or for the love, but I never imagined that I would go through this type of pain because I always considered myself the "perfect wife" and I had my stinking behavior continuously reinforced by everyone around me. How ironic!

My husband and I always got along very well, including our differences and defects, which never bothered either of us. We were always considerate towards one another, the model couple for many people. But then things changed, and he started to have an increasingly strange attitude towards me. He spent a lot of time with friends and always arrived home late on weekends. One of those weekends I woke about 7 am and he still hadn't come home and that was the last straw for me.

I ended up locking the door. I immediately regretted it and he managed to get into the house, but then the "hate wall" was already built.

We had a very serious conversation and he commented to me that he no longer loved me as before, but he did not admit that there was an Other Woman when I questioned him. Then a week passed and at the beginning of the following weekend I asked why he was acting so strange to me. It was then that he confessed that he had met someone else and that he loved her.

At that moment, my perfect world collapsed, and I couldn't believe that my model marriage was over, after all, I was always the perfect wife!

At first he didn't leave the house, but from the beginning God was warning me that he was going to leave and that I should let him go. It was about a month after my husband had confessed about the OW that he decided to leave the house to live in a flat alone, because the OW lived with her family and is a single mother.

When my husband left home I was really lost and just asked God to let me die. In one of those days of total despair I went to the computer and typed in a search engine "marriage restoration" because I needed to know if there were other couples with problems in their marriages, because I believed I was the only one who had this type of problem. In this search I found the RMI and soon filled out my Marriage Evaluation Questionnaire. Then I downloaded the book How God Can and Will Restore Your Marriage and immediately started reading it and doing the free lessons. A few days later I bought the book A Wise Woman and also started to read it.

My despair was so great that I devoured the books and lessons and started to apply each of the principles in my daily life. As much as my marriage could not be restored, I knew that at least God would make me a better person.

How did God change your situation, Lauren, as you sought Him wholeheartedly?

As at first I didn't understand where I had gone wrong in my marriage, it took me a while to realize that God wanted me entirely just for Himself.

I remember reading and rereading the lessons and not really understanding what I had done so wrong, still considering myself as the "perfect wife." Even reading the Bible, I couldn't even understand what God wanted me to do. I couldn't do anything more, I just cried and made myself a victim all the time.

The turning point was when I confessed to God about all my anxieties, fears and that I could never thank Him for my life. Of course, I felt extremely guilty for everything I said to God, but He in His infinite goodness and mercy understood my heart, wanting me to just be real with Him.

It was then that I began to feel His presence with me more and more and even hearing His voice whispering in my ear. Many, many times I felt His hand on my shoulders leading me.

I cried out day and night that I wanted and needed Him to transform my life. He claimed that He wanted me to be the wise woman written in His Word.

What principles, from God's Word (or through our resources), Lauren, did the Lord teach you during this trial?

I took the lessons and the Word of God so seriously that I used all the principles, but what I used and use most today in any situation of my life is "letting go." My goodness letting go was not easy and it was very gradual. I have always been extremely curious and of course the enemy loved to use it against me saying that it wouldn't be wrong for me to snoop here or there.

Another principle I used a lot was fasting because I really needed to learn to depend on God alone. And of course, I learned to pray and watch without ceasing as the Word says in Matthew 26:41 "Keep watch and pray, so that you will not give in to temptation. For the spirit is willing, but the body is weak!"

What were the most difficult times that God helped you through, Lauren?

I can't say that it had a more difficult moment than any other because for me my whole RJ "Restoration Journey" was difficult. I stayed away from everyone, including family members who I knew would disrupt my Restoration Journey. Therefore, I was completely in the presence of God and my Heavenly Husband at all times.

So, it was during those 4 months that my Restoration Journey lasted that God sustained me all the time and I learned to depend only on Him.

Lauren, what was the "turning point" of your restoration?

I couldn't quite figure out the "turning point", but I remember that I always prayed asking God, crying out, begging how much I wanted to be transformed and dependent only on Him and no one else in my life regardless of whether my marriage was restored or not.

Tell us HOW it happened, Lauren? Did your husband just walk in the front door? Lauren, did you suspect or could you tell you were close to being restored?

My birthday is in early March and my husband really wanted to celebrate that date with me as we always have. He set a dinner date with me and sort of asked me on a date (though I didn't consider it a date at the time).

Since the day he decided to leave the house we didn't see each other, not once, and he knew through his family and a mutual friend that I was "very much changed." Before all this happened I was always very fragile and extremely dependent on him for everything.

It was then that we set a time to meet at the restaurant and he was extremely impressed when he saw me. Despite the fact that he knew I was suffering a lot, he understood how difficult it was for me. I want you to know that I was no longer a proud woman, at no time did I take credit for who I'd become when he marveled at some change in me. Instead, each time I just made it clear that everything he saw and perceived was just the work of our Lord, my new Husband.

At the end of the dinner he commented that he wanted to return home, but he had not yet resolved his situation with Other Woman and that he would only return when he had finished everything because I deserved to have all of him fully. But it is clear that God had other plans because the next day my husband called me saying that it was over with Other Woman, she'd left him and that he would come home. Glory to God! I didn't really expect him that day but within a few hours he was home and unpacked.

Would you recommend any of our resources in particular that helped you, Lauren?

Yes of course. The materials that helped me the most were the books How God Can and Will Restore Your Marriage and A Wise Woman, the videos and the lessons.

Would you be interested in helping encourage other women, Lauren?

Yes! No question I need to share the truth with so many women in despair. God allowed this to make me A Wise Woman, to encourage women who they need to be told the truth and especially to those who have no children. Helping the childless to understand that each young woman is her daughter, her daughter who is in need of wisdom, guidance, and understanding, while boasting about our failings and how to trust God to change us.

Either way, Lauren, what kind of encouragement would you like to leave women with, in conclusion?

Do not give up, persevere and move forward in your Restoration Journey. But first of all, obey God. Pray, cry out and place yourself entirely in His presence because He will act on your behalf, you can be sure of that. Depend only on Him.

Chapter 5

Karon

"Moreover, I will give you a new heart
And put a new spirit within you;
and I will remove the heart of stone from your
flesh and give you a heart of flesh."
—Ezekiel 36:26

"We Called Each Other Husband and Wife, Knowing It Was a Lie"

Karon, how did your restoration actually begin?

To be honest, I believe it all started when our relationship began, of course, it's because it was entirely against what I knew was wrong. I am the second wife of my partner and we are not legally married, so in fact, I wasn't his wife at all and didn't know the mistake of marrying him until after our restoration. But let me begin by explaining that when I found you we had been together for almost seven years, at first he even talked about getting married but after a while he went on to say that this was not part of his plans.

Even though I was raised in a Christian home and thought I knew God, I ignored what I knew was wrong and I still accepted just living together. We called each other husband and wife, I think knowing deep down it was a lie. What I lacked was a relationship with the Lord. When we started dating, I'd been living alone for more than five years and he had been separated for two years and was living with his mother. After dating just two weeks, he moved in with me.

I have always had a very strong personality and a very explosive temper, which I thought were two fantastic qualities. It is clear that these "qualities" would be pure dynamite when mixed with a person with serious unresolved emotional problems coming from a broken relationship that left ongoing periods of drama to the mix. Due to my personality and temperament it was always me who had the final say at home. All our friends and family said I was "the man of the house." Only today do I see that that was exactly what led our relationship to ruin. But God used it for good.

We always had many fights and I always sent him away, kicked him out time after time. Then about two years ago everything got worse. I started to perceive him to be much more distant than usual and he no longer wanted to be with me. Then I received several messages saying that he had been cheating on me for some time and even with a person I knew, a woman who works with him. When I went to question him, he said it was not true but he took the opportunity to tell me that he was not happy and he wanted to separate from me because he didn't love me anymore.

This entered my heart like a sword. I was upset and panicked, over and over again I wanted to talk to him, to try to understand why all this was happening but he was only more distant with me. I started to ask God how I could solve this but at the same time I tried to solve it for myself, partly due to shame, partly due to my arrogance. No matter what, everything failed, of course because it was His plan all along.

God had broken me and was preparing my heart to receive an even stronger blow. In one of our conversations he confessed that he had betrayed me and that was consuming him because he always said that the only thing I would not accept would be betrayal. God is so wonderful that even I was surprised by my attitude. After crying a lot I just asked him if he regretted what he had done and would he do it again and he said no. So I said he owed me a second chance for us to try to be happy together. He accepted but he still treated me with a lot of indifference and he spent even more time away from home. The more I sought God for help, the more he moved away from me. Now I know that what God gave me was not what I asked but what was best for me!

How did God change your situation, Karon, as you sought Him wholeheartedly?

I was looking for books that talked about marriage restoration and I ended up finding the book "How God can and will restore your marriage." From the beginning, I realized that God was using my situation to change my hard heart.

In the beginning the more I tried to apply the principles of the book the more difficult our relationship became. After reading the book, I found the website at the end of the book, so I signed up to take the courses. He was still distant, he slept a few nights at friends' houses, and I went through times that seemed like I couldn't bear it, but gradually God began changing the situation.

After almost a year of this, I thought everything was fine and suddenly he came home one day and told me that he wanted to leave because he couldn't stand living with me anymore. He said that he was very confused and that he thought he never loved me.

Once again my heart was broken but this time I knew what to do and I had God to comfort me and instruct me. It was very painful but I stopped crying and told him that if that was what he wanted I would not object and I would not try to convince him to stay and when he left that he could take what he wanted.

He slept one night at his mother's house and the next day he called me saying he didn't know what to do and then asked me what he should do. I just answered that he should ask God and that He would show him what to do. He came home and then we went to his sister's house at the weekend but when he came back, he said he thought it was a mistake to come home. He really wanted to leave and that the next day he would take his things and move out of the house for good, I just agreed.

At the end of the next day, he sent me a message telling me that he had taken his things from home and that he wished me to be very happy and that I deserved someone better than him. When I got home I saw that he really did take all his things, and though it was painful, at the same time I felt this overwhelming peace and calm. I remained firm and confident in God and His plan, and as I said, as incredible as it may seem, I felt such a peace in my heart that I could never explain.

To my surprise, after moving on with my Heavenly Husband, I got a call from him, saying that the only way to make it right was for us to marry and that until then, God would never allow us to be happy. So he would be staying at his mother's house until we were married.

What principles, from God's Word (or through our resources), Karon, did the Lord teach you during this trial?

What God taught me during this trial was to have self-control, to be submissive to my Heavenly Husband, not to my "husband" because he wasn't my husband. I also learned to take my problems only to Him, who is the only One who can solve any and all situations, leading us to the truth as only He can.

What were the most difficult times that God helped you through, Karon?

On this journey I had several difficult moments, but the ones that most affected me was when I had to treat someone with love and patience, when it was a person who only despised me and treated me badly and at the time, mistakenly was submissive to him. Another time was when he left me very alone and when he slept outside the house and most of the time he didn't even let me know he wouldn't be coming back. These moments I only managed to overcome through the comfort of God because without Him I would not have endured this.

Karon, what was the "turning point" of your restoration?

The turning point was that my partner (who left home after almost a year of this journey) acknowledged God would not bless our union. I thought that being married would resolve everything but now I know this just created a new start to another journey I'm on now. I know there are so many more things that need to be done but God was Who turned his heart towards our relationship, returned as someone else, and asked me to marry him. Only God could do that.

Tell us HOW it happened, Karon? Did your husband just walk in the front door? Karon, did you suspect or could you tell you were close to being restored?

I never imagined that our restoration was close to happening. Especially after I'd moved on with my Heavenly Husband. One day he called and asked if I'd mind just having a simple ceremony at a church with only a pastor and a few witnesses. I said, No, I wouldn't mind because I'd never dreamed I'd ever get married. The following weekend we were married and we began our life together as husband and wife.

To be honest it took me a while to realize that the restoration that had taken place, meant that I was still an adulteress. After studying the lesson "Are you ready for restoration?" I could see that my relationship was restored but I'd also just finished Living the Abundant Life. I discovered that there are second marriages God restores, so I am not sure where I am in my journey. All I know is that I need Him more than anyone ever could and that is my life's goal. To be the best bride for Him.

Would you recommend any of our resources in particular that helped you, Karon?

I recommend all the materials of this ministry, which are clearly inspired and blessed by God.

Would you be interested in helping encourage other women, Karon?

Yes

Either way, Karon, what kind of encouragement would you like to leave women with, in conclusion?

I would like to say that as much as the situation seems impossible, for God nothing is impossible and that the more the situation seems impossible the more God will show up and take care of everything. Most important is understanding why you're on this journey, which is to know Him and to become His bride. Once you fully grasp this, it's easier to let go and trust Him.

He loves us infinitely and wants the best for us, even though in the midst of the crisis we cannot see it. Never give up, just trust HIM!!!!

Chapter 6

Clementine

"My sacrifice. O God, is a broken spirit;
A broken and contrite heart you,
God, will not despise."
—Psalm 51:17

"Being with OW Made EH Physically Sick"

Clementine, how did your restoration actually begin?

It all started with a message from my husband telling me that he was leaving. After a few days we talked because I didn't understand what was going on and that's when he told me that he was no longer sure of his feelings for me, that I was suffocating him and he just did things for me and had stopped thinking about himself and needed time for him to think. After our conversation he decided to come home but then he said he couldn't do it anymore and I let him go. My world collapsed that day, I thought about how I could even live without my husband, how I could be a separated mother, a woman abandoned by her husband. I saw no hope for anything, I thought I had done my best and could only see his defects. I sought help from pastors and friends, but no one gave me hope.

How did God change your situation, Clementine, as you sought Him wholeheartedly?

One day I started searching the internet about marriage restoration and found the book How God can and will restore your marriage. I read each page, not believing what I was reading, and as I read it over and over God was showing me the foolish and arrogant woman I had become. I dropped to my knees and surrendered everything to God. I told Him I wanted to be completely broken and restored. I told God I wanted Him to use my life as He wished and I was willing to obey the Lord's will for me in everything.

After a month I discovered RMI and started my journey! God showed me His infinite love, took away all the hurt, pain I felt for my husband and taught me to forgive. My husband did not want to talk to me anymore and whenever he came to pick up our daughter he showed that he no longer cared for me. I prayed for him every day and wished he wouldn't ignore me because it hurt (it didn't just hurt me it hurt our daughter). Over time I gave everything to God and let Him do what only He can do. I just kept obeying and seeking more and more of His presence. I no longer felt empty and I was happier than I'd ever been in my life when He became my HH, I no longer spent the day thinking about my husband and my days were all focused on my Husband.

What principles, from God's Word (or through our resources), Clementine, did the Lord teach you during this trial?

God taught me that I should let my husband go and not get in his way. At first I chased him and didn't leave him alone, but then your ministry showed me that I shouldn't get in his way. After that my husband told me that he had an OW, I was at peace because you had already shown me to be prepared. Of course I was sad because we had only been separated for a month but I handed him over to God and did not criticize him or say anything negative. I was always kind towards my husband, even though he treated me with indifference and sometimes rudely, yet, I always received him with affection, meekness and love.

What were the most difficult times that God helped you through, Clementine?

The most difficult moments were when my husband went to live with OW and on the weekends he took our daughter to stay with them. These were the times I suffered a lot but I handed everything over to God and asked for His will to be done. I prayed that God would put the hedge around my husband and also for Him to give new life to OW by restoring her family. It was very difficult to know that my husband was with her, but my HH strengthened me and taught me to trust God's plans, which are much bigger than mine.

Clementine, what was the "turning point" of your restoration?

My turning point was when I understood that only HE could satisfy me and love me, that I truly only wanted to be with my HH and that I could be happy, happier than I'd ever been in my life. I asked Him to help me let go of everything that kept me from being fully His, which was my husband and church mostly. I realized how wonderful it would be if my marriage was not restored, as I would have time only for my HH and dreamed this to come true. I asked Him to remove my husband from my heart and as I stopped praying for him by handing him over to God for Him to do His will, that's when everything changed. When I let everything go and I had the peace that God gave me that surpassed all understanding.

Tell us HOW it happened, Clementine? Did your husband just walk in the front door? Clementine, did you suspect or could you tell you were close to being restored?

My husband took our daughter to spend the weekend with him at the OW's house, I was sad but then realized all the time I could have with my HH. Once I decided that I would use this time to spend more time with my HH, He led me to fast, pray specifically. To once again declare that I wanted His will, that I wanted to just obey Him and live His will. To ask again that He not allow my daughter to go to the house of OW, to touch the heart of my EH so that he would not want to take our daughter to that house, but above all to finish my prayer by declaring His will to be done and not to mine.

Well then, He did His will and not mine, my husband took my daughter and I just obeyed. To my surprise before he brought my daughter, he stayed at our house and he still slept here with me. We were intimate for the first time after three months and to my surprise the next day he decided to return home. He told me that he couldn't stop thinking about me, about what we had together and the damage he knew he was doing to our daughter. That day we reconciled, he told me that he no longer wanted a relationship with OW, being with her made him physically sick. That day he left to pick up his clothes when he knew she'd be out and left her key on the counter.

I never imagined that this would happen, because my husband was cold and distant the entire time! He never came into our house, he just stayed at the front gate. He didn't call me and everything seemed to point to living a life without him. But God was in control and it was at that moment that restoration was no longer my focus that God turned my husband's heart back to me.

Today our marriage is nothing like I ever dreamed and it's all thanks to You, my Love!

Would you recommend any of our resources in particular that helped you, Clementine?

I recommend the book how God can and will restore your marriage, this book made me see the truth about the woman I had become—all based on God's Word. Your courses and all your resources really.

Would you be interested in helping encourage other women, Clementine?

Yes

Either way, Clementine, what kind of encouragement would you like to leave women with, in conclusion?

Never give up on your marriages, however difficult it may be, God never forsakes His children. When everything seems unsolved and we don't believe that anything can change, when we let everything go and focus on our relationship with our HH, that's when God comes in and transforms the impossible situation. Seek the Lord and give everything to Him. If you withhold anything from Him you only lengthen your journey. Do not be anxious but seek only your First Love.

Chapter 7

Astrid

"But let it be the hidden person of the heart,
with the imperishable quality of a gentle
and quiet spirit, which is precious
in the sight of God."
— 1 Peter 3:4

"I Always Thought that if I Ever Wanted Him Back, He'd Be There!"

Astrid, how did your restoration actually begin?

First, I want to say that all of my testimony is for the honor and glory of the Lord! Without Him, His immense love and mercy, none of this would be possible.

It all started when I got married young, very immature, with little idea of what a marriage really means. I only considered the wedding and not how to live as a wife. And with no sense of being a "wise woman" as you can imagine, my husband and I fought A LOT, over small things, all the time. I didn't know how to shut up. I didn't know how to speak kindly. I always wanted to be right and I didn't accept "backing down" in any discussion.

The fights were really terrible and each time I opened my mouth, I pointed out all his defects, being blind to mine (there were so many!). Besides being contentious, I never took pleasure in taking care of our home, being a woman of God who builds her home, caring for others and even wanting children, I was like every woman in this fallen world we live in.

My husband always complained about it but I (knew) I was right, saying that I was not his employee! (Absurd!!!). Well, time passed and we were coming close to our 2 year anniversary. Due to failed contraception we had a child, a son and when our son was 1 year old, in another one of our heated discussions, I started to tell myself and God that I couldn't take marriage anymore! I didn't know what else to do. That I didn't want him in my life anymore and I felt lost.

A few days later, situations started to happen that I thought were "signs" God was showing me to separate! (How naive!). I did not know that God NEVER wants a marriage to be broken, that God hates divorce and that was not His will, but what I wanted! Well, a few weeks later, I (who was already super cold and distant to my EH), asked my husband to leave the house. It wasn't what he wanted, but he left. He asked me several times to rethink, to try again, saying that marriage was forever, that he loved me. And I, completely blinded by sin and hardened in heart, did not listen.

I think it was about 3 months later that he really wanted to come back and I said, no way. I filed for divorce. However, the lawyer sent it incomplete and we had to redo it. When we went to redo, I kept the papers in my car, and I didn't close the door right when I got home and it rained. All the papers got wet! And I kept putting it off and thank God this divorce never happened! Glory to God! He was already working in our lives.

After a year of separation, with one failed divorce attempt after another, my Nana asked me to take her to church. As I was sitting in mass, I told God that I was feeling lost, I asked Him to do His will in my life, that I was giving my life in His hands. Suddenly, everything started to make me want my marriage back! I never imagined this would happen to me. To want to do everything differently!

I really wanted to live together again and take care of our house with pleasure! I looked at my son and cried thinking how I was able to destroy our family! How blind I was! So I thought that when I went to talk to my husband, he would want to come back and we could remake our little family.

When I said, I'd like to talk! He looked like someone else! Extremely cold! He said he didn't want to have anything to do with me, that things had changed, he spent a lot of time thinking it over and that he was enjoying his life and that today he had peace he didn't want to lose! I got scared! I always thought that if I ever wanted him back, he'd be there!

In a rage, I began to insist, tell him he was cruel, told him to come to church with me, sent him scriptures, but nothing, nothing worked. On the contrary, he felt increasingly distant and completely indifferent, more resolute in his decision. He told me he had no one, he just didn't want to come back, he couldn't imagine himself with me anymore. One day I saw a conversation with a "friend" on his cell phone. I asked who he was talking to, he was very angry that I touched his cell phone, and said that I hadn't changed as I'd claimed. We fought again and he was even more distant, if it was possible.

How did God change your situation, Astrid, as you sought Him wholeheartedly?

After that, I texted an apology, he was cold in reply. I kept looking for reasons to talk to him all the time. I went to talk to a man from my church and he prayed with me, calmed me down and encouraged me not to give up. I said that God would restore my marriage. I remained steadfast in prayer. I cried many, many, many times at the Lord's feet. With each cry, with each prayer, I felt transformed, I felt closer to God. I went through a real conversion, I started wanting above all to do the will of God, to follow His Word, to want to be closer to Him and do what was pleasing to Him. I was changing as a person, not only dealing with my marriage, but with everyone in other situations. I thanked God for the opportunity to be a new woman, for His mercy, for calling me to be close to Him even having sinned so much! I kept thanking Him for His transformation, even though I didn't have my marriage back, I was becoming a new woman.

It finally took a turn when my husband and I were talking about how to handle the holidays. Every year he travels to another country to be with his family and he wanted our son to go too, but because he was little, he couldn't stay long. So he proposed that I go with them. I was happy and accepted! I thought that's when our restoration would happen and that we would return as a couple. How wrong I was, I got so frustrated a few times, but I quickly turned to God, knowing that His plans were better than mine!

What principles, from God's Word (or through our resources), Astrid, did the Lord teach you during this trial?

"All things work together for good for those who love the Lord and are called according to his purpose".

"Letting go" and "gentle and quiet spirit" are what's important!

What were the most difficult times that God helped you through, Astrid?

This trip lasted a full month and a half and can I say that at times it was very difficult?! Quite different from what I imagined it would be. My husband remained completely cold, distant and indifferent towards me. He showed absolutely no desire to return to our marriage or show the slightest interest in me. I felt really bad and rejected because we were altogether in such tight quarters and with his family.

Many times he would leave me there with our son and go out with friends, go to neighboring cities, in short I was there as a nanny for his son. At times I despaired, but I knew God used this time to humble me. I'd been nothing but arrogant and self-centered and God needed to break me fully so I never went back to the way I'd been!

I began to think of it as impossible, that perhaps God did not want to restore my marriage. I asked my HH to support me, because I couldn't take it anymore! Every time I said that, after crying a lot and talking to God, I felt renewed and had the strength to continue. Until one day I put "restored marriage" on google and found RMI. It was what I needed! I downloaded the book "How God can and will restore your marriage" and started reading. Everything seemed to fit! I had already regretted the separation, but after starting to read the book I understood all MY mistakes during the marriage. I was ashamed. How contentious I was! I was unbearable, disobedient. I also tried to restore my own marriage rather than letting God do it.

Astrid, what was the "turning point" of your restoration?

When I started to understand my mistakes and learn the principles of shutting up, letting go, that changed me even more. The situation seemed the same, but I started to feel a lot of peace while reading the book, a lot of faith and a lot of certainty. I believed it would happen in God's time, and He did plan to restore my marriage. It was only up to me to obey and wait and allow Him to finish transforming me. I couldn't force anything or try to do anything on my own, such as make charges in me I knew needed changing.

The book was the one that completed my prayers, then I found A Wise Woman and began rebuilding my life and my mind on His Word. When

I combined my prayers with the principles I learned, things started to change!

Tell us HOW it happened, Astrid? Did your husband just walk in the front door? Astrid, did you suspect or could you tell you were close to being restored?

So, still on the trip, after more than a month of being away, while he was gone and I was at home, reading the Bible, studying lessons, pouring my heart into my journals, when he called me and asked if I wanted to go out with him. I was sooo scared! I had so much peace that I wasn't expecting it to happen! I said I would, so he came to get me and we left. And there he told me that he wanted to try again, that now he could imagine a new life with me. He proposed that we still not live together, and I accepted, saying "I agree, I'm not ready." He gave me a kiss and when we came back to his parents house we were holding hands! I was very happy!

However, in the following days, he remained cold and distant. I could not understand why. It hurt me, but I didn't want to be ungrateful, not only to him but mostly to the Lord. So I went on thanking and praising the Lord, knowing that there was a reason for this return to his old feelings towards me.

When we got back from the trip, we talked again and that's when he told me that he really wanted to try, from the heart, but that he was not managing to be as he was, that despite wanting his family back, he was not managing to feel anything for me, not the way he'd thought he would feel and really how he wanted to feel towards me. I felt very sad about this, but I continued to thank God and ask Him to turn my husband's heart to Him and then to me.

That's when he proposed that I come to live with him, and I did. Our son was so happy! And I started to put into action what I wanted our home to be built on. Caring for our home made me so fulfilled. I followed workers@home and got good at being a homemaker, a far cry from the woman who tore her own house down. I didn't force anything, I didn't charge anything. I kept going out to be alone with my First Love. We lived a bit like "strangers" in the same house, but despite a few moments of sadness, I was at peace and enjoying my Beloved Husband. Thanking and praising God became what I did all the time.

I knew it was the beginning of a restoration. Looking back, after 3 months of prayers for my restoration, we had already arrived, we were restored, it just wasn't what I'd imagined. Yet I was thankful and I rejoiced even more!

Then a few days later, there was a crisis in my EH's life and he started to get closer to me to reach out to me for support. He became affectionate. A day or two later, on Sunday, he asked if I'd go to church. There was a prayer group at the church he took me to and he asked if I'd go. When we walked in a man came up to pray for us, he said after praying, "God says your marriage has already been restored! Your crisis is over."

After that day, which will be three months this weekend, everything changed! Everything! He is someone else and we are much more spiritually involved in our new church. He said that since that day he sees me again as his wife, as someone who completes him! I know we are still on our journey and we must always remain in prayer, praise and thanksgiving because the Lord still needs to work hard on both of us! But this time our house is being rebuilt on the Rock of His Word, and God is at the center of our marriage! God is perfect, my sisters! His timing is perfect and His works are perfect too! Trust! It seemed impossible to me ... and it really was! But with God NOTHING is impossible and He granted me this MIRACLE even though I didn't deserve it! My Beloved, I LOVE YOU !!!

Would you recommend any of our resources in particular that helped you, Astrid?

How God can and will restore your marriage, A Wise Woman. The Bible.

Would you be interested in helping encourage other women, Astrid?

For sure!

Either way, Astrid, what kind of encouragement would you like to leave women with, in conclusion?

Stand firm in the Lord! Look at the Lord and not the circumstances. If I had looked at the circumstances, I would have given up, because everything seemed to be going the other way far from restoration. But our God works miracles when we give everything into His hands and trust! Trust! May the peace of God triumph in your hearts!

Chapter 8

Breona

"It will no longer be said to you, "Forsaken,"
nor to your land will it any longer be said, "Desolate";
but you will be called, "My delight is in her,"
and your land, "Married"; for the Lord delights in you,
and to Him your land will be married."
—Isaiah 62:4

"I am Surprised at the Courage I Had"

Breona, how did your restoration actually begin?

I discovered RMI in February 2016, as I was searching the internet, looking for testimonies of relationships and marriages restored by God. One day the Lord led me to Erin's testimony and I was led to the French site aidemaritale.com. That same day I think I read the first two chapters of Restore your Marriage. I was so relieved and excited! That was exactly the answers I needed! And I knew deep in my heart that it was God who led me there.

Before that I was completely broken and desperate. I had broken up with my boyfriend after almost two years of the relationship. I was so ignorant, such a fool, and so proud…I wanted to have my way and I was contentious.

Everything was running so well at the beginning but then the gap between my boyfriend and I got bigger with time. I didn't want to lose him so I started pursuing him with my "love". I focused my intentions and thoughts on him. The more I tried to please him and to be close to him, the more I made him angry. He eventually told me that I was stressing and pressuring him. Later I discovered that he did not consider wanting to marry me. I felt neglected and despised, and I became very contentious. I suspected he had focused his attention on another woman so I started snooping on his phone, his emails and his Facebook. I found out that he had always been in contact with his ex-girlfriend, that they were again very close and that he had even sent money to her.

We were living in a foreign country and I eventually had to go back to our home country. Out of jealousy and pride I decided that I should be the one breaking up. Though I was very irritated with my ex, I knew I had messed up a big time but I didn't know how to fix things. I suffered and cried a lot for months. That's when I turned to the Lord. I told Him that despite all that was happening, I could feel in my heart that it was not over between my ex and I. That I had tried everything I could but I had failed. I told Him that I knew I had reached my limits, but what was impossible to me was possible to Him.

How did God change your situation, Breona, as you sought Him wholeheartedly?

As I sought the Lord wholeheartedly He convinced me of my sins. I had always labeled myself as "Christian" but I discovered later that I was just religious. I knew very well that having a boyfriend and living with a man without being married was a sin. I tried to convince myself that it was not that bad and I was somehow comforted since nobody I knew condemned my lifestyle. Nevertheless, I was never really happy in my relationship because of my inner conviction. I was living in sin but I didn't want to stop the relationship as I was hoping it would lead to marriage. I created a huge gap between the Lord and me. I was not able to pray, to pour my heart to the Lord. The result was that I stopped trying to please the Lord and I instead focused on pleasing a man.

The Lord showed while reading the RYM and Wise Woman books that I was a true Pharisee. Always pointing at others' sins and ignoring or minimizing mine. Concerning the relationship I cherished so much, I was now able to see where exactly I went wrong.

The Lord also taught (is still teaching) me humility through various trials. Believe me beloved sisters, I never knew how proud I was before starting this restoration journey.

Finally, the Lord convinced me that it was Him that I needed to be restored, that I should seek Him first. Dear sisters, it's not very easy because many times I get distracted by my circumstances. But I can assure you that each time I fully focus my attention on the Lord I witness Him fighting and winning my battles.

What principles, from God's Word (or through our resources), Breona, did the Lord teach you during this trial?

The first truth the Lord revealed to me was His great Love. His love and forgiveness healed and literally saved my life. His love is unconditional; He did not wait for me to become a perfect person to love me.

The second principle I've learned is that I can win people without a word. I didn't have to say what I think. There is no need to protect and defend myself by arguing with anyone. I should go with my concerns to Him. Only He is able to put compassion, understanding or love in someone's heart.

The third principle is tithing. I have always tithe since my first salary but I didn't know I had to give to the Lord first. I also didn't know that I was to tithe in my storehouse. I used to tithe where I would see a need.

What were the most difficult times that God helped you through, Breona?

God helped and is helping me a lot through my loneliness. It's been almost two years that I have been living alone.

I know, even if I sometimes complain that He is my faithful Companion. Loneliness has never worn me down to the point where I will desperately look for a man to fill an emotional void.

I used to cry to Him at times begging Him to make a way, so that I will at least live with a family member. He consoled me and I am still living alone. And oh, how I needed to be with God and myself! The Lord made me look at myself in the mirror during this time. I needed healing, yes I badly needed to be restored. I wanted Him to restore me to a boyfriend, but I didn't know how broken I was inside. I had experienced trauma in my childhood and I did not know how affected I was. I did not know how much my character was influenced by these abuses. I had no idea how much of my personality traits were anything but normal. My soul needed healing.

I experienced moments of deep depression, discouragement, sadness, anxiety and unexplained fear. But the Lord has always been by my side. He taught me that no other presence except His could free me from those demonic feelings.

Breona, what was the "turning point" of your restoration?

The turning point of my restoration was when the Lord began slowly, but surely to open my eyes to the reality of my situation. The Lord kept speaking to my heart and repeating to me: you are not married to this man!

It may sound silly to you, but it was a revelation to me. I felt like I had scales falling from my eyes, as if I had lived in darkness for a long time.

I declared with my mouth that I was single, each time I filled in official documents or even my journal at the end of each lesson, I checked the box reserved for single people. But my heart lived another reality. My soul was deeply attached to this man.

The truth is that I would not have sought God's help if I saw what I had experienced with my ex as a harmless adventure; like a story I could draw a line on.

I was living like a woman waiting for the return of her husband.

Tell us HOW your Restoration finally happened, Breona?

Now that I knew how wrong I was in my relationship with my ex, the Lord began to show me how much I had idealized my ex. He helped me name character traits from my ex that I didn't see when we were dating. Whenever my ex contacted me, I suffered terribly because I felt that he had not changed his attitude towards me; the worst part was feeling that he dangled a carrot before me and that he expected me to chase him.

The Lord also revealed to me that I did not love my ex as much as I thought. He made me realize that I was held in guilt and shame. I still regretted having been intimate with a man who was not my husband (I had always wanted to know only one man) and I thought that it was no longer possible to meet someone else.

Not at all. In fact, I never thought that things would happen this way. During this period when the Lord was opening my eyes to the truth, my ex began to become more and more insistent and even began to flirt! He who sent me text messages once every three months, had started to contact me every month and then every two weeks. Then came that week when he called me every other day and that day when he asked me if we could chat by video call.

It was exactly what I had dreamed of for years, what I had prayed and fasted for. However, after this rapprochement, I knew that I knew it was over. Even today, as I write my testimony, I am surprised at the courage I had to block his number so that I would no longer receive his calls and also delete photos of him that I still had. After that, I literally felt a weight leave me, I felt after that that the Lord had freed me from all impurity. The most wonderful thing is that I felt that from now on I could love God with a whole heart.

I had long dreamed of the day when I would write my testimony of restoration. When I arrived at this Ministry, there was no testimony from a single woman. In September 2017, I wrote in one of my journals "I am aware that the principles of this book are primarily intended for married women, but I am happy because I know that my testimony will be unique. It will serve to evangelize." I, myself, am very amused by this statement I made. Yes, my testimony is different. To be honest, I was far from imagining that my testimony would look like what I am writing at the moment.

I thought that since I was not married to my ex, that I should wait to testify of my restoration when I get married according to the plans of God. This testimony is long overdue. But to wait to testify means to give little importance to the transformation that God has brought about in me.

I'm restored, hallelujah! Restored to my Heavenly Father who teaches me to see myself as He sees me. Today, I am more and more aware of my identity and my value in the Lord. I am engaged to Christ, who paid a great price for my dowry. God loves me and I have a price in His eyes.

Today, I don't just want a wedding. I want a marriage that glorifies God in the eyes of all who know my story. And this marriage will be the subject of another testimony :)

Would you recommend any of our resources in particular that helped you, Breona?

The book "How God Can and Will Restore Your Marriage" is simply a blessing. You may wonder how I can say it when I have not married my ex, but the Word says that God speaks sometimes in one way, sometimes in another (Job 33:14). So yes, He spoke to the single woman that I am by this book. He used it to remind me with delicacy but firmness that He was My First Love.

He used this book to teach me about His will concerning marriage. He used it to change my heart and prepare for the wedding He planned for me.

Do you have favorite Bible verses that you would like to pass on to women reading your Testimonies? Promises that He gave you, Breona?

Isaiah 62:1-2 (NASB)

"For Zion's sake I will not keep silent, and for Jerusalem's sake I will not keep quiet, until her righteousness goes forth like brightness,

and her salvation like a torch that is burning. The nations will see your righteousness, and all kings your glory; and you will be called by a new name which the mouth of the Lord will designate."

Isaiah 62:4 (NASB)

"It will no longer be said to you, "Forsaken," nor to your land will it any longer be said, "Desolate"; but you will be called, "My delight is in her," and your land, "Married"; for the Lord delights in you, and to Him your land will be married."

Isaiah 62:6-7 (NASB)

"On your walls, O Jerusalem, I have appointed watchmen; all day and all night they will never keep silent. You who remind the Lord, take no rest for yourselves; and give Him no rest until He establishes and makes Jerusalem a praise in the earth."

Isaiah 62:11 (NASB)

"Behold, the Lord has proclaimed to the end of the earth, say to the daughter of Zion, "Lo, your salvation comes; behold His reward is with Him, and His recompense before Him.""

Would you be interested in helping encourage other women, Breona?

Yes

Either way, Breona, what kind of encouragement would you like to leave women with, in conclusion?

The most important in this walk is to listen to the Lord, to seek Him in relation to our own situation. I know from experience that it is not the most obvious thing. It is sometimes very frustrating to see that things do not happen for us as for others.

Above all, remember that God led you to this Ministry because He has something special for you. This Ministry is a Ministry of Restoration, so be sure that you will be restored. God bless you.

Chapter 9

Cordelia

"Enjoy life with the woman whom you love all the days of your fleeting life which He has given to you under the sun; for this is your reward in life and in your toil in which you have labored under the sun."
—Ecclesiastes 9:7

"My Sister, Restored, Began Encouraging Me"

Cordelia, how did your restoration actually begin?

Just days after we got back from our honeymoon, my husband disappeared on a Sunday after he said he was off to fly a kite. He didn't bother inviting me and then he didn't come back home until it was well after dark. From that moment on I realized that he did not want to be married. The desire was just to have someone to live his life and bring him contentment, without the worries or responsibilities of being a husband. One day, I was ill and stayed home from work. I had horrible back pain but rather than stay home to help me, without saying he was leaving, he just left me to go play ball. I was very upset and in my anger I took some pain medicine and just got busy cleaning the house. For hours after he came back, he just sat on the sofa relaxing. I was frowning but didn't say anything hoping he'd apologize. He finally asked what he could do to help me and I was fighting the urge to just lose it and scream at him. He saw the state I was in, so he nervously said he was leaving and would come back when I was in a better mood. So I grabbed his arm and ended up hurting him.

My many reasons for why I had assaulted him just made him more angry, so he simply left and took all his clothes! I remember crumbling right there on the floor and crying to our Lord, I opened the Bible and the Lord brought me to 1 Samuel 2:1 [Hannah's Prayer of Praise] Then Hannah prayed: "My heart rejoices in the Lord! The Lord has made me strong. Now I have an answer for my enemies; I rejoice because you rescued me." So I stood up and began rejoicing, praising Him with thanksgiving.

By the Lord's mercy, the next day he returned home, but the fighting didn't end there. I will briefly say that twice God spoke to me that the pain would be great and the tears would be great, but everything would be difficult in the beginning, but if I would let Him change me, in the end, we would be restored for good.

My sister and I became ePartners on that day because we were experiencing many difficulties in both our marriages. So I started going to her house to pray and in the same week, my husband left again moving to his parents' house. At that same time is when I found the RMI ministry and let him go. I did not say anything. My pastor went to talk to him and everything that the book, How God Can and Will Restore Your Marriage said he repeated, telling the pastor that I was: contentious, quarrelsome, and a huge Pharisee! Glory to God, for showing me this and I knew God was giving me the opportunity for a spiritual transformation, to become a new woman, wife, sister and daughter.

How did God change your situation, Cordelia, as you sought Him wholeheartedly?

First, I looked for a church that believed in restoring marriages. For nothing is impossible with God and He hates divorce. After that, I asked for prayer on an Internet site and that's when someone sent me the book How God Can and Will Restore Your Marriage by email. I searched the Internet more and found the RMI site.

I devoured that book. I read it at work during my breaks, during every bit of spare time I had, and put everything into practice as far as possible. Later, I received information from my pastor that my EH called with the intention of returning home. I was very happy, but it still took a couple of days for him to call me and say he was coming back. Later I discovered that he had already filed for divorce. He'd contacted a family member who's a lawyer. Later I discovered he never even referred to me by name but simply called me the "problem." Since he does modeling besides his regular job and said that the "problem" (referring to me) just wasn't worth stressing over.

Even though he was adamant about divorcing me, in the end, God prevented him from filing the papers! The day his cousin called me, saying she was sending someone with the papers, I replied that the next day I'd be here and would happily sign. I'd just read how important it was to agree and agree enthusiastically in the facing divorce again book, so I trusted God and did what it said without reservation. I told her I would contact her once I signed them. Then right after hanging up, I called my sister who I knew was suffering. My brother-in-law left her because he had fallen in love with a woman who lived in another city. He was a salesman and he was always away offering "his services" to women as he went from city to city. But during one of his regular stops, he met this particular OW. There was a long period of time when he'd come home reeking of her perfume. My sister would be so horribly upset, she'd make him sleep in his car, which caused him to despise my sister.

So I called to encourage her, to share as many principles I could, reading from the book several the pages I had highlighted and shared how I happily agreed to sign the D papers. My sister said I shouldn't, that I should fight it but I told her, no, God will fight for me so let's just begin to praise Him for all that we both were going through

What principles, from God's Word (or through our resources), Cordelia, did the Lord teach you during this trial?

During that time of so many trials, my sister and I got together more and more in prayer and then doubled our time rejoicing, dancing before the Lord, thanking Him for our trials. I cried to my HH in secret sometimes because I was worried about my sister. I told Him to show me that this would pass and at least as a sign, to please do something for my sister who was the one really struggling. Soon afterward, GOD brought my brother-in-law back home and I watched God do it. That's when my sister, restored, began encouraging me, because my husband had still not returned. My faith was high and so I focused more on making my time alone count for more than just focusing on myself and what I knew...that I could simply trust God to do what He'd promised.

What were the most difficult times that God helped you through, Cordelia?

The most difficult thing was when my husband called saying that he would never return after he heard my brother-in-law had returned. Then he told me he'd met another woman he was modeling with and they were better suited to each other. Almost the very next day she showed up on all of his social networks and changed her last name to his and uploaded dozens of pictures of herself with him. It was the same day that God delivered my miracle to my heart. I wasn't meant to see all of this, it was someone at work who ran to show me and before I knew what I was looking at, the enemy had made his way in.

So I did as I always did and praised Him even more, knowing that if it was this intense God was battling and needed my praise to win the victory for me. Praising Him was my part.

Cordelia, what was the "turning point" of your restoration?

With God nothing is impossible! When my husband returned to his mother's house to stay the night, he went to his boyhood bedroom and opened the Bible that was still on his nightstand. And for the first time since he left home, He opened his Bible after He heard God speak to him. He said he opened the Bible to Ecclesiastes 9:7. "Enjoy life with the woman you love, every day of this meaningless life that God gives you under the sun; all your meaningless days! For that is your reward in life for your hard work under the sun."

Tell us HOW it happened, Cordelia? Did your husband just walk in the front door? Cordelia, did you suspect or could you tell you were close to being restored?

I understood that my fight was coming to an end because it had become so difficult. I had no idea what had happened to my husband, but I knew I'd praised God so it was very, very close.

I spent Friday night as what I believed might be one of my last days alone with just me and my HH, so I wanted to cherish it. The very next morning, my husband called me and said he had prayed on Wednesday and God had spoken to him through the Word. How beautiful, because just the night before I'd opened to that same verse and highlighted it. That day I prayed to ask God that my husband would return to rejoice in His goodness with me.

Well, he came back that same Wednesday, five months ago and we began by thanking God for His goodness and faithfulness to us. My sister and I continued together in prayer because her marriage wasn't restored fully. I told her she needed to let God work and that her part was to praise. I told her that God was committed to those who were committed to Him and that He contemplated us both in the early morning, throughout the day, and as we slept. That if we trusted His purpose, our God would honor us. And so He did.

My brother-in-law asked my sister for forgiveness right after God closed the door on his job. Because he was unemployed and without a vehicle, we knew he would not be able to continue his normal life. We simply witnessed what He was doing while we praised Him. Then we heard that God told my brother-in-law that he needed to want another job, a job to which he could return to his wife each night. How beautiful is our God! Now he is a different man.

As far as my testimony, God continues to work on both of us. Months after my husband returned, he confessed that he cheated on me, not with just one person, but with several. He said he was sorry, and yes, even though it was difficult he was thankful because things between us became good! God used it all for good.

Would you recommend any of our resources in particular that helped you, Cordelia?

How God Can and Will Restore Your Marriage and the Holy Bible to start. Prison to Praise and Facing Divorce Again.

Would you be interested in helping encourage other women, Cordelia?

Yes

Either way, Cordelia, what kind of encouragement would you like to leave women with, in conclusion?

It is not by force, nor by violence, but by my Spirit, says the Lord. Praise, praise, praise Him rather than begging and worrying because that quenches what He's promised to do. Let go and let God restore you. Because if you do, the One who started the good work will be more than faithful to finish the work He started. Think of others more than yourself. Don't just strive to restore your own marriage, find someone else and watch their marriage restoration to build your faith. We simply must believe in His goodness!

Chapter 10

Martina

"Truly I say to you, whoever says to this mountain,
'Be taken up and cast into the sea,'
and does not doubt in his heart,
but believes that what he says is going to happen,
it will be granted him."
—Mark 11:23

"I Honestly Wanted to Commit Suicide"

Martina, how did your restoration actually begin?

It all started when my partner, that's right, partner (because I wasn't legally married and before coming here I wrongly called him my husband) went to live in another state. I didn't go with him, he didn't ask, he just left and when he got there he called me.

Betrayals began to be uncovered, not just his but also on my part. And because of many fights not only did he leave, but I began being unfaithful to our relationship.

Since I was raised in the church, my family is very religious but no one followed the principles of the Bible. But the Lord knew my heart and knew I was very sorry. So I agreed to get married soon after (he'd asked me many times but I refused) and when I got married I wanted to build my new marriage on the Rock.

This wasn't what my EH had in his heart though, and soon after we were married he began avoiding me, staying on different sides of the house from where I was and I also noticed he started to lie a lot. He was gone most weekends and because he worked way out in the country, he often just stayed there rather than commuting back home (usually spending three days or four days away from me).

Soon I realized he was involved with another woman, then another! The first time it was very painful but my EH did not leave the house. I was prepared to divorce him but instead I studied all day to take my mind off things, and even when he'd be at home I was always studying and did not give him any attention. It seemed the more we talked, the more we fought and I was tired of it. I prayed and asked the Lord to please just resolve everything. He did.

After what happened and just when I thought that everything had normalized and peace would reign in our home, once again the enemy hit me hard, this time my EH was involved with two different OWs within a three-month period. What was worse is because knowing that he and I have no children, one of the OW had her children call my husband "daddy" which was the worst blow that anyone would give to a person who's longed for her own children for so many years.

The OW used his kindness and love for children, to make him believe they were his children. When I thought it couldn't get any worse, I heard from someone that she had become pregnant! I honestly wanted to commit suicide at the time.

Anyway during this entire drama, right in the middle of it, my EH gets involved with a second OW. Later he told me he worked with this woman and began to open up to her. He told me he couldn't tell me anything because he was so ashamed so this woman offered a sympathetic listening ear. He told her that my dream, besides getting married, was to be a mother and he also told her about the dream of us together of having a son and how I had continued working and how we had postponed having children so that he could give money to help his family (that he still helps).

In the end, throughout it all, through this terrible part of my journey, through all the trials in my relationship, I stayed in prayer and asked our Beloved to help me uncover everything that was hidden and wrong in my relationship with Him first.

How did God change your situation, Martina, as you sought Him wholeheartedly?

The Lord transformed me in such a way that even I did not recognize myself. In all the many situations that I mentioned above, I would never have been able to control myself before, but this time I was different, I was transformed.

First, my Beloved helped me have a gentle and quiet spirit, reminding me to always look to Him. In the beginning I would pray and fall on the floor begging my Beloved, but as soon as He became my HH, things were different. My faith was no longer very small, nor did I pray with doubt. The more I gave myself totally to the Lord and gave Him all of my heart, trusting His Word without doubting anything, soon great faith emerged, and I'd watch as everything would begin to be resolved with no effort or pain or worry or anything on my part.

I started to have such a very deep peace that I had never felt before or knew I could feel. Ours is something very special, my Beloved and I! I started to give my entire restoration over to our wonderful God, my Father, so I could just be a bride. I always thought that one day my testimony would help others like me, women forsaken and following religion, lacking a true relationship. I just can't tell you how I feel right now that this day has come.

After I gave myself to our Beloved and asked Him to do everything according to His will in my life, I remained faithful and followed what the book asked me to do. I fasted, I agreed with my adversary, I let go, I did my courses daily, pouring my heart into each one. I cooled myself in the water of the Word.

I read HOW GOD CAN AND WILL RESTORE YOUR MARRIAGE more than three times over several weekends, and then began going through each of the Abundant Life courses.

Each day after my time alone with Him, I'd go immediately to your website and I'd do one or more courses. I sent in praise reports. As soon as I was being completely obedient is when everything happened. I began ministering to other women and boy it's then that I went through trials! But rather than back away, I knew it was the Lord who was testing me and because of His love, I was able to keep myself still and quiet and allow myself to be humiliated and didn't defend myself, but kept entrusting my reputation to Him who judges righteously.

I am very grateful to Erin for her book, for her devotion to her ministry even though so many have come against her. I know it's because she is helping so many women like me. Thank you so much for everything!! For not giving up or giving in. "Friendship with the world is hostility toward God. Therefore whoever wishes to be a friend of the world makes himself an enemy of God" (James 4:4).

After I came through this, my Beloved brought me to live close to my husband who had moved into the country (it is where we are living now) and it's when I discovered that there was no child. The pregnancy was a lie. My GOD had resolved everything, and I thought we would be at peace. But no, the enemy wasn't done with me, with us, just yet.

Again the same OW told everyone she was pregnant, posting an ultrasound picture on Facebook, so he left me after he asked me to move in with him. It was the longest separation we'd had, a full three months. She pressed him in every way but I was calm and thankful I had more time to be with my HH and to have nature all around me; where I could feel Him even more than when we were living in the city. I simply trusted in the Lord and followed through with obedience and my husband soon returned.

What principles, from God's Word (or through our resources), Martina, did the Lord teach you during this trial?

The principles that helped me was to let go. If I hadn't, I wouldn't have been able to embrace my HH with my whole heart and being! When I let go completely I started to see the transformation in me and watch GOD take care of things that really seemed impossible. At first it was not easy, because I could not let go of my husband especially after we'd just married and the more I saw other women claiming to be his. I needed to really press into Him, and told my HH that unless He did it "in me", I would never get what I wanted most, which now was Him!

Another very important principle for me was to be meek and quiet because before I could not control myself and all I did was talk, talk, talk and that led to fights and more fights. I always wanted to win in everything, I was a very contentious woman. It was fasting that tamed the shrew. I was too weak, as Erin says, to react and say something. These two principles were paramount to my transformation. The principle of keeping silent running only to my HH was also paramount. Because before I opened myself to family and friends and got more and more lost and confused. Once I started to open only to my HH my world changed.

What were the most difficult times that God helped you through, Martina?

The most difficult times that the Lord helped me through was right after my EH asked me to come to live with him and then he left saying his girlfriend was pregnant. I was alone out in the country, far from my family. Yet He used it for good because that's when I learned to run to our Lord and kneel down and cry. Soon I was not crying but praising.

Oh, also early on when I thought about suicide but the Lord helped me was a very difficult time. When I started to pray constantly, read the bible out loud and follow all that Erin was talking about in the book and videos I felt a lot of inner peace. I chose life! I read this part of her book over and over:

This is the time to choose. "I call heaven and earth to witness against you today, that I have set before you life and death, the blessing and the curse. So choose life in order that you may live, you and your descendants, by loving the Lord your God, by obeying His voice, and by holding fast to Him; for this is your life and the length of your days . . ." (Deut. 30:19–20).

Martina, what was the "turning point" of your restoration?

The turning point was when I had my Love and wanted no other. He has sustained me and given me everything I wanted but didn't know I wanted when I began my journey. I want only Him. I came for a restored marriage, for the pain to stop, but when I got Him, when I wanted only Him, I got everything and so much more!!

Tell us HOW it happened, Martina? Did your husband just walk in the front door? Martina, did you suspect or could you tell you were close to being restored?

It happened suddenly one day. I came back from a short trip to visit my family. When I got home there were two children, two small children who I thought were his children (from the OW who weren't his children). It caused me to stop in my tracks, but then in my heart I praised Him. That's when I saw it wasn't those children, but children from two of his friends from high school who'd come to visit. When he saw me he jumped up, gave me a hug, and told me to go grab a shower because we were going out.

As I was getting ready, my husband came in with a bunch of trash bags and his backpack full of his clothes. He didn't say anything to me, he just grabbed me in my towel and he asked me for forgiveness! When I looked in his face I realized he was different. He told me his friends showed up soon after he'd prayed and asked God to help him. His friends were Christians and when they asked how he'd been, he told them everything, confessed everything. They prayed for him and he said he had felt such a peace and the huge burden he'd been carrying was gone.

I'd decided right from the beginning of my journey that I would not tell God how I expected everything to happen, not my will but the Lord's will and do it just how He wanted it. As Erin says in her testimonies, books etc. that God will do it His way, so I just assumed there would be no repentance and I was fine with it. I trust the Lord who I knew would transform my EH heart at some point.

Soon after we were together, I found out I was pregnant and very soon we will have our first baby, it's a boy. Everything I went through, it was necessary to be transformed and I thank the Lord so much for all of it. For every heartache, for every trial.

Would you recommend any of our resources in particular that helped you, Martina?

Yes! I recommend the book as God can and will restore your marriage, read the daily devotionals, read the Bible over and over and over again, read the day's psalms and proverbs, take the courses, read the testimonies, watch the videos and be sure to give your tithe to your storehouse. Just obey the principles. Write all the verses that Erin recommends, fast to be gentle and quiet and make Him your first love!

Would you be interested in helping encourage other women, Martina?

Yes

Either way, Martina, what kind of encouragement would you like to leave women with, in conclusion?

My beloved brides and fellow companions in this restoration journey, my words of encouragement to you is that you go ahead with great faith and do not give up. Follow everything Erin says with great obedience because today I am the one who has had my relationship restored but tomorrow it will be YOU for sure. Therefore continue to persevere, believing, fasting because if you do, it means your restoration is closer than you think.

Proverbs 3:5-6

"Trust in the Lord with all your heart and do not lean on your own understanding. In all your ways acknowledge Him, and He will make your paths straight."

Then Jesus said to the disciples, "Have faith in God. I tell you the truth, you can say to this mountain, 'May you be lifted up and thrown into the sea,' and it will happen. But you must really believe it will happen and have no doubt in your heart. I tell you, you can pray for anything, and if you believe that you've received it, it will be yours. (Mark 11; 22-24)

Chapter 11

Victoria

"My son, do not despise the Lord's discipline,
and do not resent his rebuke,
because the Lord disciplines those he loves,
as a father the son he delights in."
—Proverbs 3:11-12

"This Time I Decided I was Going to Kill Myself."

Victoria, how did your restoration actually begin?

My husband and I had problems in the marriage from the beginning. I always criticized him about everything, for me everything he did was wrong and I was right. I tried to talk about our problems and it always ended up in a fight. I always looked for reasons to criticize him, and he'd try to change but no matter what he did I was not happy about it. I felt like a victim, and I suggested to my husband several times that we split up, because I thought we had made a mistake getting married. But he always wanted to work to make things better.

In October, I started to feel depressed all the time, my world revolved around my husband, he was my priority, and not God. In November, I really concluded that I was in a true depression, and I became even more dependent on knowing what my husband was doing on his social networks, accusing him of things that had no meaning, that I just imagined. My husband emotionally distanced himself from me, and he no longer cared when I fought with him, he didn't try to change as before. Anyway, I asked for a divorce, because the lies in my head took over and consumed me, but what I didn't expect to happen, happened! My husband accepted the divorce, he didn't try to change my mind like he had done before. I ran out of ground, where to run to next and tried to start another fight, reminding him of several things he had already done and also hinting at several things that I'd long forgotten. Then, the biggest shock came, my husband told me that he didn't love me anymore!

This catapulted me into a mad woman, I acted like I shouldn't have acted, I screamed, I fell to the floor proving I was the victim, I accused him, but he didn't care anymore. During this time I decided I was going to kill myself, because I didn't want to live, I couldn't accept what was happening in my life, but something always stopped me and it was God. Hallelujah! Glory to Him because, Lord, Your promises have been fulfilled in my life.

After this episode, I went to spend a few days with my mother-in-law. To stop me from killing myself, my husband reluctantly had said he would give our marriage one more chance. While there I begged and manipulated him so much, we ended up fighting even more and reaching the conclusion (with the help of my mother-in-law) that we should separate for a time, and I should leave. I cried all day and couldn't stop thinking about it, until God took me to Psalm 119, and while I was reading God brought me hope. I was not looking for hope, because it seemed impossible to me, but as I was reading that day God gave me that Word, and spoke to my heart. I told my husband that I didn't want to be separated anymore, he didn't agree, but he welcomed me home again anyway.

How did God change your situation, Victoria, as you sought Him wholeheartedly?

On the day I read Psalm 119, I went to the bathroom and prayed to the Lord asking Him to deliver me from all depression, for I knew that He alone had all the power to heal me and deliver me from what held me to these horrible thoughts of death. There I decided to give myself to the Lord, to die to myself so that He might live in me. I asked for forgiveness for all my sins and began to seek the Lord. That night, for the first time in months, I managed to sleep well, I had no insomnia. Then, I realized that God heard me and was answering my prayer.

I started reading Christian books on marriage and applying what I read, it started to transform me. My husband picked me up at my mother-in-law's house, and when we got home, he was very cold and distant. During the whole drive, he told me he was not happy being with me, and he would never be, that I should stop and think that maybe God didn't want us to be together because otherwise, we would not be going through all of this. Of course, it hurt me, but I knew it was the enemy lying to him. I insisted on talking to him about our marriage, how we could make it better, when all he wanted was for me to leave.

One day I was on the internet looking for testimonies of restored marriages when a testimony caught my attention. She was talking about the book How God can and will restore your marriage so I immediately looked for it and started reading it. When I started reading the book, God broke me and showed me everything I had done wrong in my marriage and what I was still doing wrong. I asked God for forgiveness and started applying the principles of the book in my life. As I did this, I saw God transforming my husband. He started telling me that he knew that God's will was for us to stay together, but he still didn't feel anything for me. My husband no longer tried to hurt me, and when he did he apologized. I flung myself at the Lord's feet over and over. I felt the love of God in my life and no longer argued with my husband, just being quiet brought back peace to our home and relationship. Every day God renewed His strength, joy, and peace in my heart and I learned to be content in every situation.

What principles, from God's Word (or through our resources), Victoria, did the Lord teach you during this trial?

All the principles I learned from the Word of God and the resources of the RMI I applied to my life. But it was essential to "let go" of my husband, to get out of his way so that he had space and breathing room. Once I did that the hate-wall fell, and we started to have a friendship. He told me that he was already happy with me at home, but that he still didn't want to be with me.

Another fundamental principle was to acknowledge my mistakes to my husband and ask for forgiveness, something I have never done since we were married. I confessed my sins to him, and to the people to whom I had spoken ill of about my husband. I asked for forgiveness and told everyone the mistakes I had in the marriage, assuming total guilt.

What were the most difficult times that God helped you through, Victoria?

The most difficult times were when my husband said that he did not love me, that he would not be happy living with me because his happiness was by not being with me. When he said that he wanted me to leave, and that he did not plan to be with another, but probably it would someday happen and I should be prepared.

It distressed me a lot, but I talked to God and everything passed, it disappeared as if it had never been said. God enveloped my heart with His love and grace, and gave me more and more of Him so I could forgive my husband. In all of these moments, I was strengthened by the Word of God, and I stood firm on my journey with Him because He did not leave me alone. At no time did He leave my side, He was true to His each of His promises! Hallelujah! Praise the name of the Lord for this and so much more!!

Victoria, what was the "turning point" of your restoration?

When I returned home, God led me to fast for 21 days. In my heart, I knew He ordered this, and I obeyed. In those 21 days, God led me to stay away from all social networks and soap operas, which were an addiction for me.

When my fast was about to end, God put in front of me all my sins and the mistakes I'd made during our marriage and used me to confess this to my husband. So I did, I obeyed the Lord, even though I thought the consequence would not be very good. My husband was angry but said he forgave me. He ended up telling me about some of his mistakes during those times when we were separated, but said he still had more. In my mind, I concluded that it was an OW. I prayed to God to get it out of my mind, but if it was true, that He would bring out the whole truth and prepare me to forgive.

The next day God showed me that I had forgotten to tell my husband one of my sins, because I thought it was less important. But I ended up confessing to my husband because I wanted to be obedient to God, and what was least important to me was not a small thing for my husband. He was very, very angry, he yelled at me a lot and at the end of everything, because of his anger, he confessed that he had betrayed me, in order to hurt me, which he had denied until that day. I was prepared, and I said I forgave him, even when my husband said he didn't regret it.

Anyway, I totally let my husband go and told Him that I was going to leave him alone, not because he had betrayed me, but because I didn't want to get in his way. I told him that I wanted to see him happy, and I didn't want to get in his way. I gave everything to God and asked that

His will be done in this whole situation, that He would take me where He wanted and take care of my husband.

The next day, when my husband and I went to bed, my husband said that he admired my attitude of having asked for forgiveness from everyone to whom I had shamed him, and said that I was very strong for putting up with everything I was going through. Then, he started to cry and asked me for forgiveness for all the words he had said the night before, he said that he was sorry for being with the OW, and that it was just a kiss, that he'd led me to believe it was more because he wanted to hurt me. Then he said that he was confused by this whole situation, that he had seen my change, and that he wanted to be with me, but at the same time he was afraid of our future.

Tell us HOW it happened, Victoria? Did your husband just walk in the front door? Victoria, did you suspect or could you tell you were close to being restored?

At the end of the 21-day fast, I gave everything to the Lord, and the next day I was going to leave. It ended up going wrong for me to leave, my husband ended up arguing with my brother about it and I was a little distressed with this whole situation. My husband was working and said he wouldn't take me to the bus station that day, and when he got home we were going to talk. He came home and I didn't ask anything, I waited for him to say something.

We left to grab dinner, and on the way we got into the subject of my brother having a fight with him, I was upset about it and I ended up venting about it, and saying that he should also understand my brother, then I asked his forgiveness for saying something that hadn't pleased him. After that, he said he was going to change some things. When we got home, he hugged me and kissed me. I said I was confused by that, so he told me that he didn't want me to leave. Since that day he never brought up the subject of me leaving, nor have I, and said he wanted us to work to make our marriage work. I praise God that even when I fell, He was faithful and kind to me, turning my husband's heart and using it to put my husband in the place of being my spiritual leader.

This happened in late December, and I continued to remain steadfast in my new marriage. It has been much more difficult for me since my husband "took me back", but I have remained in God. At the end of January, my husband again said that he loves me, another prayer answered, like all of them God is always faithful and answers all prayers!

Now, I wait on God for my husband to be in His presence again and to want Him more than he wants a good marriage. And I praise Him because I know that He has all the power to do that!

My marriage has been better than it has ever been. My husband has been very affectionate, loving, and kind to me and our children, as he has never been. God brought balance to our marriage the moment I became humble and my husband stepped into the position of being our spiritual leader. We are very, very happy together, and because God is for us it doesn't matter what comes against us!

Would you recommend any of our resources in particular that helped you, Victoria?

I recommend the book How God Can and Will Restore Your Marriage, each of the RMI courses, read the Praise Reports daily, which was what I used most to keep myself stronger along with devouring the Word of God and in constant prayer with thanksgiving. They all helped me to remain steadfast in my hope and certainly guided me to reach my restoration. God used this ministry to restore not only my marriage but my sanity and my relationship with my HH.

Would you be interested in helping encourage other women, Victoria?

Certainly, of course. I ask Him to guide me every day to reach out and tell people about hopeatlast and share my testimonies, so that other people who go through situations like mine can find hope.

Either way, Victoria, what kind of encouragement would you like to leave women with, in conclusion?

Never give up on your marriage, however impossible it may seem, for God nothing is impossible. He is our only hope, and believe that He does want your marriage to be restored, even if everything seems to shout otherwise. He is guiding you into the desert to show you His love and transform you so that you can enjoy an abundant life in Him, and a marriage based on His Word.

God is calling you to be His bride, and for that, He needs you in the desert land for a while to be alone with Him. But, as soon as you are ready He will restore your marriage. So, move ahead on your journey, wait on the Lord and see victory coming in His hands!

"And that's not all. We also celebrate in seasons of suffering because we know that when we suffer we develop endurance, which shapes our characters. When our characters are refined, we learn what it means to hope and anticipate God's goodness. And hope will never fail to satisfy our deepest need because the Holy Spirit that was given to us has flooded our hearts with God's love." Romans 5:3-5

Learn to be content with the situation in which the Lord placed you, for it was necessary for me to have been afflicted so that I could learn the decrees of the Lord (Psalm 119:71), and love Him with all my heart as He longs for you to do.

Today I praise You, my Beloved, for all that You have done in my life and in my marriage, and for the transformation that I see happening every day in my husband. Dear bride, believe, God is faithful!

Chapter 12

Luciana

"And my God will supply all your needs according
to His riches in glory in Christ Jesus."
—Philippians 4:19

"I Hadn't Gotten Married Only to Separate"

Luciana, how did your restoration actually begin?

It all started when my husband started treating me with indifference,
saying that he didn't love me anymore and that our marriage was over.
He kept on tormenting me, always saying he was leaving, until one day
I got home from work and he had actually gone and taken some of his
things. He left a note saying something like this: The Lord has helped
us so far!

As soon as I read that I told God that I did not accept that situation, that
I had not gotten married only to separate.

**How did God change your situation, Luciana, as you sought Him
wholeheartedly?**

The Lord began to transform me the moment I started to acknowledge
my mistakes and repent. Taking responsibility for all the problems that
I contributed to the breakdown of my marriage was only the first step.
I didn't know (until I found your ministry) that I was quarrelsome,
contentious, and utterly a fool. I simply said anything and everything I
thought. I was also a Pharisee and religious with no relationship with
the Lord whatsoever.

I thought I was the right one, I wasn't humble, never took the blame for
anything even though I was usually at fault. It was when I found your
ministry and took one of your courses that I learned that we must ask
God to show us where we are going wrong, and also to ask Him to give
us the opportunity to ask for forgiveness before I would soon find
myself before a judge. Matthew 5:25

What's interesting is that after I started to pray like that, when I began to cry out to God to show me where I was going wrong, He started to show me and I started to be ashamed of myself. Until I was farther along in my journey and began reading your Living Lessons and learned that shame isn't from God. At that point, I knew I needed to be reshaped and remade by our Father and when it really happened in my life, when I found my HH, I was able to see and feel God's love and that of a true Husband.

What principles, from God's Word (or through our resources), Luciana, did the Lord teach you during this trial?

The principle of letting go and to depend exclusively on my HH. Oh, what a wonderful experience! I started to watch the supernatural of God take care of everything I needed. I didn't lack anything, because He met all my needs.

What were the most difficult times that God helped you through, Luciana?

The most difficult moments for me were when I found out that he left home to live with an OW, but I cried out to the Lord and He cherished me with the following verse. "Even if my father and my mother forsake me, the LORD will welcome me" Ps 27:10

Luciana, what was the "turning point" of your restoration?

The turning point was when the Lord, my HH, became everything. Almost immediately God began to turn my husband's heart back towards me. The hatewall came down (because in my heart I let go to grab hold of my true Lord). One day my EH said he dreamed of me every night and was feeling the urge to seek me out to ask for forgiveness, to buy a house so we could live a new life together.

Tell us HOW it happened, Luciana? Did your husband just walk in the front door? Luciana, did you suspect or could you tell you were close to being restored?

My husband left home but he didn't take all of his things. Our God transformed my life and that of my family. He is a God who creates adversity in order to bless us. As Erin says, very often our miracle comes in the midst of a crisis. Without any warning, we found out we were in a flood zone and were told we needed to move, immediately. I contacted my EH asking to come quickly to get his things, because I was going to move that day. I decided to take only what I needed and leave the rest.

As soon as he was finished, he offered to take a few boxes I had packed and sat ready at the door. Then just as I locked the door and chose not to look back, my EH was there and asked me if I would meet him at a cafe so we could talk. We talked and that's when he told about the dreams he had about me, that he never stopped loving me, that he was desperate after not finding me on social media (thank you RMI!) and that I am the woman God put in his life and we were meant to live together until death do us part, that we have an alliance and he wants to have children with me (music to my ears).

Rather than move into the shelter, he moved my things in with his, at his brother's house. Two weeks later we found another small flat up on a hill.

Psalm 40:2—

"He brought me up out of the pit of destruction, out of the miry clay, And He set my feet upon a rock making my footsteps firm."

Would you recommend any of our resources in particular that helped you, Luciana?

Yes, I recommend the books How God Can and Will Restore Your Marriage and a Wise Woman. I read these books several times and this is how God spoke to my heart. I also recommend fasting, prayer and reading the Word of God. All of your courses were amazing. I still do at least one lesson a day.

Would you be interested in helping encourage other women, Luciana?

Yes, I am very interested.

Either way, Luciana, what kind of encouragement would you like to leave women with, in conclusion?

Beloved of the Lord! Don't give up on your marriage, I was very humiliated but the Word of God says that the humiliated will be exalted and the Lord exalted me. Perhaps you are praying and thinking that nothing is happening anymore, but our God works in silence. Today I see how it was worth it to be obedient to God and obedient to studies, to put everything that we learned here into practice, to close our mouths, to leave social networks, not to want to know where the husband is and with whom he is. "Give your way to the Lord, trust Him and the more He will do". Ps 37:05

He is faithful! He watches over His Word. He is not a man to lie, nor the Son of man to repent. Numbers 23:19 "So that all may see, and know, and consider, and together understand that the hand of the Lord did this, and the Holy One of Israel created it." Isaiah 41:20 All honor, glory and praise to Him!

Chapter 13

Maisie

"But I have this against you,
that you have left your first love."
—Revelation 2:4

"He Broke Down Weeping and Asked for Forgiveness"

Maisie, how did your restoration actually begin?

It started after the Lord restored my marriage the first time. I foolishly walked away from my first Love and started to focus on my marriage and EH, instead of continuing to look to my Beloved for my needs. This led to me returning to the contentious woman I'd been. In short, I returned to want things my own way and in my time and not in God's time. So HE thought it best to "remove lover and friend from me" again, and within minutes I wished I had that intimacy with Him as before. I regretted not taking the time to be with Him and the distance in my relationship with Him that resulted in me blaming my EH and wishing I'd never let him come back inside my heart. I blamed the EH for the distance between me and the Lord. When my EH came back, I didn't have that peace anymore so I wished for it to be different but in the wrong way, I was ungrateful to the Lord and became demanding again.

One day I arrived home from work and for a trivial reason, I discussed my unhappiness with him. He told me the same thing, that he was not satisfied with me either, he retaliated and decided to leave the house again. I couldn't blame him after I had time to see how I'd been acting.

Today I know it was the Lord who removed him, to teach me to be grateful and trust Him and to wait on Him and that the completion of restoration doesn't depend on me but on His will, the Lord's will, and His timing. Then in my arrogance, I thought that now I knew how to do it and that it was just to seek the Lord and move on, it crossed my mind that I now could do my way and not the Lord's. I thought I could manipulate the Lord, how silly I was!

How did God change your situation, Maisie, as you sought Him wholeheartedly?

It allowed me to go through things that I never imagined, that I would go through. I will not give details because what matters is to glorify the Lord, yet there were very difficult moments. I was reluctant to continue my journey that was much harder than the first time, then I realized that it was useless to be afraid and that I had to trust the Lord. A day or two later, after such a long time without being able to feel that peace and the Lord's hand, I knelt down and felt a little of that peace, feeling the way I felt the first time. That day, even in the midst of great pain, I decided to simply seek the Lord, to seek His presence.

At the same time I was in His presence, I received a message from my EH, as he didn't speak to me in the message, I called our son to listen to the message from his dad. He wasn't speaking, he was crying, but I didn't care because I was feeling such peace and His love and wasn't drawn to my EH at all. Clearly I'd let go deeply in my heart again, so once again God turned his heart and that's when he called me. He asked me how I was doing, something he didn't do anymore, so I knew it was God letting me know I was headed in the right direction again. I don't remember exactly what he said because I was half-listening but I think he said he was coming to have lunch with me and our son. He came and we had a nice lunch, and though he was trying to mend things and hint towards coming home again, I didn't promise anything or try to get him back. When he left we were more boyfriend and girlfriend. He reminded me how he'd wanted this once before but I behaved badly because I still had hurt feelings and voiced my mistrust.

First and foremost, what was most important and what I knew I needed was to have time to get close to my first Love, because to go right back to being together would mean I would be the same contentious woman again and I simply didn't feel ready for his return, so I was reluctant because I was afraid of going through everything again and again. This led to my EH begging me to start over and he even cried when I said that I wasn't ready yet that something inside me needed to be changed. I was so shocked that I trusted Him so much to not jump at having my EH back. My only concern was to not lose the stability that the Lord had given me, just thinking about me and making sure it was going right for me, I couldn't see the Lord who was in control, so I continued to seek the Lord and because of my selfish and arrogant attitude I suffered a lot after that because I thought I had to beg for Him to help me with so many situations, which I now recognize wasn't necessary. He was in control and all I needed to do was rest in Him and keep my focus on Him.

What helped the most was going back to doing my lessons, seeking the Lord first. I began to learn to live with expectancy, trusting the Lord, not doing anything in my own strength. I learned that it was of no use being afraid or wanting to run away, or to beg Him when His love covered all of that.

What principles, from God's Word (or through our resources), Maisie, did the Lord teach you during this trial?

Letting go, whatever the stage or situation, I had to let go. Die to myself, not want my will. I had to apply this principle again and again. I have to apply it every day. I also learned the principle of overcoming evil with good, loving, and praying for our enemies, the principle of submission in a new way. I learned the beauty of waiting. I learned never to murmur or complain, I learned contentment in all things. I learned the principle and power of staying in agreement.

What were the most difficult times that God helped you through, Maisie?

The hardest was when I had to see him with OW, and not react, but to instead be kind. After the first time the Lord let me know she was contentious, and soon would become bitter, but then my son told me she was always quiet and nice, so it hurt hearing that.

The other really difficult time when I was almost losing hope was when he sent a message saying he was going to file for divorce. But I knew I had to agree, and shortly after that, I was hit hard again when I had to see my son and her daughter playing happily. The Lord comforted me and showed me how much I had changed because I felt compassion for them.

Maisie, what was the "turning point" of your restoration?

After all that I had come through, the Lord comforted me, I spoke with HIM that I would not like to go through divorce, that if it was possible for me to pass that cup, but that it was not my will but HIS, and I knew that even if I had to go through this and that if HE was with me and that everything would be fine.

Then one night I felt a great emptiness so I went to look for the presence of the Lord, and that's when I saw a message from my EH asking if I was okay, and if our son was okay. I was surprised because when he wanted to talk to his son, he called. I said that everything was fine with us. Then he asked me if I felt anything for him, I was afraid to respond so I asked him to send an audio because I began thinking that it could be the OW; she'd sent texted from his phone to me before so I wanted to be wise and remain gentle, Matthew 10:16 "Behold, I send you out as sheep in the midst of wolves. Therefore be wise as serpents and harmless as doves." He answered in audio, when I was sure it was him, I replied that of course I felt something for him. So he told me that he was not well, and he was just about to go to take a shower and come to sleep here at home if I would I said yes. I said yes, of course. That was on a Sunday night, I prayed and went to sleep.

I asked my HH to give me peace if it was time for Him to restore. I didn't want to create false expectations or fears. Before he came he called again, asking if we were needing food, he said he was going to bring milk, so I thanked him, then our son got on the phone and asked to go stay with him in his apartment. He said he was not well, that he was very sick, and when he was better he would talk about everything with him. I just thanked My Beloved because only He was able to turn someone's heart in our favor and I saw He was using this sickness for that purpose. He was not only turning my husband's heart towards me, but my heart towards him as well. A day later he sent me an audio asking me to come and bring our son so I went.

Tell us HOW it happened, Maisie? Did your husband just walk in the front door? Maisie, did you suspect or could you tell you were close to being restored?

Our son and I went to his house as he had asked, arriving there he said he would come home with us, so it was three days and nights when he was sick, staying at our home, and the Lord lovingly was taking care of him through me. My EH even said he could feel it was the Lord who was caring for him. At one point, he broke down weeping and asked me for forgiveness.

No, I didn't suspect anything was about to happen.

Would you recommend any of our resources in particular that helped you, Maisie?

Your lessons, books, daily encouragement, and the Bible are vital to understanding the restoration process.

Would you be interested in helping encourage other women, Maisie?

Yes

Either way, Maisie, what kind of encouragement would you like to leave women with, in conclusion?

Dear bride, you must trust in Him and in His promises that He is faithful to keep. You don't need to beg or worry or try, just leave it to Him. Even when it seems that there is no way He changes the situation, do not give up, seek the Lord, put Him first, and obey, He never fails, He knows the time and the way through every difficulty. Give up your way and just trust Him. The more you let go the more He will do. What is impossible for man is possible for God.

Chapter 14

Bernadette

"Because God is the one who works in you both
to want and to do, according to his good will."
—Philippians 2:13

"I Carried the World and Its Worries on My Shoulders"

Bernadette, how did your restoration actually begin?

I am writing this testimony after much inner struggle. I am still ashamed that I am not officially married in the church but I still felt it was important to praise, magnify, exalt and glorify my true LOVE, the One who was, who is and who is to come. Hallelujah!!! I'm so thankful for all He has done by helping me understand that I should marry, not live pretending I am married, for turning the heart of my partner to want to ask me and then accepting his proposal all due to the Restoration Journey He called me on and walked with me on!

At the appointed time, I know that my Beloved is going to give me a beautiful wedding, in the meantime, my Heavenly Love and I are encountering an even more intimate relationship.

When I arrived at RMI, I came from years of misunderstandings and breakdowns, following various advice, and being carried away by different teachings, where people misused the gospel that were nothing more than lies, lies I believed. When I became a teenager and sought the Lord for the first time, I studied, I went to seminaries, I took a pastor's courses, I even held positions in the church and yet I was ignorant to the truth about marriage. The entire church is ignorant of what God's Word actually says because no one is encouraged to read the Bible for themselves, but worse, to not make having a relationship with the Lord as the most important thing that they teach. Something that all women long for, to feel in love from their Heavenly Husband.

I grew up without an earthly father, my mother got married several times and "whoever" would become the "man" of the house in the absence of my mother who was always the financial provider. Because of this, I became rude, bitter, irritable, overly concerned with everything and even when everything seemed to fall apart, I thought I had to fix the mess. I carried the world and its worries on my shoulders.

A few years ago, I started a psychology course, which was one of my life's dreams along with having children, training leaders, having a home, and my own ministry. I pressed forward with all my strength, and that's when my world started to collapse. I walked away from the church and met my partner, my son's father. When I got pregnant, he came to live in my house as he had also just recently left the church and turned away from the ways

After our baby was born, we moved to another city, and I went back to church. It is important to clarify that I soon became even more bitter when the spiritual leaders began to press me to get married. I threatened my partner and after a big fight, we went on for another year and a half without intimacy, me holding out as a threat. I thought that I could force him to marry me in this way, and I could thus get "right" with the church and church leaders. I never did it for the right reasons or with the right heart. And as expected everything went wrong. A great crisis occurred and we had to start living in separate cities, with him returning to his mother's house and me living at my family home. He came to visit our son once a month, and although he helped with expenses, and was patient and showed respect and a little affection towards me, I discovered some of his unfaithfulness and started to not care. I told myself I needed the status, MARRIED. I didn't want to be seen as an abandoned, single mother. Everything was becoming a burden and there was no shortage of people who advised me to abandon this guy and move on finding someone new. I am not talking about people in the world, but people in the church and my church advisors.

As I said above, I learned at an early age to carry the world on my shoulders, and naturally take on all the responsibilities. I used to tell everyone that I had two children (my partner and our son). I was quarrelsome, contentious, the queen of knowledge and all truth, a Pharisee, full of self-righteousness. I finally came to the point of having my partner come to gather his things and never come back. Only then did I realize that I was following the path my mother took, what I witnessed as a child, that I was going to leave my son without his father, keep finding new men, that I would continue to be bitter and overwhelmed. So because I didn't want to see my son go through what I went through, and be raised by a bitter and contentious woman, the breadwinner, bringing in one new "dad" after another, I cried out to God to show me the way, to help me find the truth and that's when I discovered RMI.

How did God change your situation, Bernadette, as you sought Him wholeheartedly?

When I came to RMI I immediately took the Finding the abundant life course and met my LOVE for the first time. I knew Him as my authority and Savior but no one told me of the Love I'd been missing. The Husband I needed and the bride I needed to be. Also the Father that I'd desperately needed in my life!

The day I found Finding the Abundant Life, I knew He called my name, He showed me that He still cared about me and I felt so guilty. I begged, cried, asked Him to come to me again and do whatever was necessary for His plan to be fulfilled in my life and in the lives of our family. After I found that I didn't need to beg Him and finally understood His love for me. I started taking the courses on marriage and I realized how wrong I was. So as Erin teaches, I immediately called my partner and asked for forgiveness for my behavior and for how I had behaved up until then but with my newly-found relationship with the Lord as my Husband, I hoped to change.

Day after day, teaching, after teaching, reading How God Can and Will Restore Your Marriage a dozen times in the same week, and was shocked that I started to struggle with my behavior, again. Until my Love showed me that I had already fought too much and tried to do everything myself. I asked my Darling to teach me, to mold me, to help me to really have the meek, gentle and quiet spirit. Then people started to be used to test me, so I ran to Him and poured myself out, and kept quiet while fasting to kill my flesh. I started to study the Word daily and instruct my son in the ways of the Lord, teaching him everything I was learning. We memorized verses and recited them together every day.

I realized that I no longer trusted my leaders, who did not see that although what they taught wasn't in God's Word at all, so I started reading A Wise Woman to learn how to be a wife, a mother, a daughter, and as I was taking this course, I began to study the various testimonies of restored marriages and share the daily encouragement with a friend who was facing a personal crisis. She faced a crisis in her marriage, including physical abuse (this I hope to share later, how it stopped once she had her relationship with her Heavenly Husband and exhibited a gentle and quiet spirit causing conviction on her Earthly Husband who no longer abuses, praise be to God).

I let go of EVERYTHING, my fears, anxieties, self-pride, the desire to finish the psychology course, which had already been interrupted twice and confirmed later when I did the psychology lesson. I knew it was Him sparing me from ingesting more lies. I learned not to justify myself and turn the other cheek and also the power of fasting to be able to give my life completely to the Lord, without reservations, without panic, without being anxious.

What principles, from God's Word (or through our resources), Bernadette, did the Lord teach you during this trial?

It began with finding my Husband while taking Finding the Abundant Life, then I studied the books How God Can and Will Restore Your Marriage, A Wise Woman, and then passed on the encouragement, devotionals, videos and courses to women I met.

What were the most difficult times that God helped you through, Bernadette?

When I realized that I had destroyed the family that I always dreamed of for my son because I never wanted a husband or a marriage. Also, the difficulty in learning how to submit and be emotionally healed.

Bernadette, what was the "turning point" of your restoration?

It happened when I let go of the fear, the shame and just shut up and stopped commenting on everything. The burden fell from my shoulders.

Tell us HOW it happened, Bernadette? Did your husband just walk in the front door? Bernadette, did you suspect or could you tell you were close to being restored?

It happened the day that my partner came to our son's school party and brought his parents. He asked for forgiveness and sought intimacy with me, which I said would come later. That day we reconciled. That weekend we went to the courthouse and were officially married and although we were not married in the church before God, we are a family who attests to the promise in Joshua 24:15 "...as for me and my house, we will serve the Lord."

Immediately after that, everything began to turn in our favor, we started planning a move to the same city where my Earthly Husband works. We moved back and live in the same house again, but this time I am without a job and I'm a worker@home. At this point we had no idea how to pay for our son's school but since coming to RMI. I have always been faithful in tithing to my storehouse and since then, even in the midst of a "financial crisis" in the country where we live, I have increased my tithing to include an offering even though I had not received a salary we have all the money we need—proof that tithing works! ~ Bernadette "I Carried the World and Its Worries on My Shoulders"

Ah, our Beloved does not allow us to be ashamed, and now that I am no longer an abandoned woman, I know that I am His beloved bride, I can rest easy knowing that He will orchestrate everything without any effort from me.

When we moved in, when we were all living together, I let go of church, but my husband goes while I stay home to teach our son the ways of the Lord. Because I don't work, I can go to school with my son and I am at home to educate him when he comes home. I have everything ready for my husband when he comes home, the house is in perfect order by studying workers@home. Most importantly, I have a set time for me and my BELOVED. Because I have no income, I spoke to my husband about tithing to RMI, the storehouse who has been feeding me, and PRAISE GOD he has set aside a separate tithe to give to RMI for feeding me who is feeding my son! He also gives a portion to the church that is feeding him.

I know that my situation is not the RMI norm but I know that there are so many women who are living with their partners, being advised by leaders to leave them and find someone new because they are not married, and to destroy the family when there are children who will be left without their father. Only after rereading the instruction again for those who never married legally did I discover the testimony that opened my eyes Married to my Son's Father. I hope you will write more for women like me as it seems that your material is written for single women, without children.

Of course, this is because everything has changed so much in the world and the church is not helping women like me with this trend. What made the most difference is when I wanted to be married, when the idea of marriage was no longer a mystery once I found my Love and my Heavenly Father. I wish so much that I had included marriage as part of my dreams, to have a husband. I thought it was a needless accessory to have children, but then not wanting to be a single mother and to be ashamed, most do as I do and make themselves self-sufficient and felt as I said, not needing a husband, just a new father for my son when you get fed up with the last one.

But now I want to honor my Beloved through my marriage, and to teach women that the husband is the head of the wife, as Christ is the head of the Church. I am trusting Him day after day, for us to show others what He wants for us. I know that the Lord will complete the good work that He began. Darling, I am Your beloved Bride and I live just for You.

"Neither eyes have seen, nor ears have heard, nor has it ever penetrated into a human heart what God has prepared for those who love him." 1 Corinthians 2:9

"Because God is the one who works in you both to want and to do, according to his good will." Philippians 2:13

"Like a stream of water is the king's heart in the Lord's hand; it tilts you wherever you want. Every man's path is straight in his eyes; but the Lord weighs hearts." Proverbs 21:1-2

Isaiah 54:1-14—

"Sing joyfully, O barren, who have not given birth; rejoice with joyful singing and exclaim, you who have not had labor pains; for the children of the lonely woman are more than the children of the married, saith the LORD. Enlarge the space of your tent; spread out the awning of your dwelling, and do not hinder it; lengthen your ropes and secure your stakes well. For you will overflow to the right and to the left; your posterity will possess the nations and cause the desolate cities to populate. Do not be afraid, because you will not be ashamed; do not be ashamed, because you will not suffer humiliation; for you will forget the shame of your youth and you will no longer remember the reproach of your widowhood. For your Creator is your husband; the Lord of hosts is his name; and the Holy One of Israel is your Redeemer; he is called the God of all the earth. For the Lord has called you as a helpless woman with a low spirit; as the woman of youth, who has been repudiated, says your God. For a brief moment I left you, but with great mercies I received you again; In a rush of indignation, I hid my face from you for a moment; but I have compassion on you, says the Lord, your Redeemer. For this is like the waters of Noah to me; for I swore that the waters of Noah would no longer flood the earth, and so I swore that I would no longer go against you or rebuke you. For the mountains will go away, and the hills will be removed; but my mercy will not depart from you, and the covenant of my peace will not be removed, says the Lord, who has compassion on you. O thou, afflicted, bold with the storm and disconsolate! Behold, I will set your stones with colored mortar and will set you on sapphires. I will make your bastions of rubies, your doors, of carbuncles and your whole wall, of precious stones. All your children will be taught by the Lord; and your children's peace will be great. You will be established in justice, far from oppression, because you will no longer fear, and also from astonishment, because it will not come to you."

Would you recommend any of our resources in particular that helped you, Bernadette?

Yes, EVERYTHING.

Would you be interested in helping encourage other women, Bernadette?

Yes, it's the only way to really live the truth by sharing it with others.

Either way, Bernadette, what kind of encouragement would you like to leave women with, in conclusion?

Seek the Lord, let HIM reflect His face on you, let go of all deception, walk away from the lies even if it means leaving the church. Trust Him to teach you, don't let all that you know about Him be by what others tell you, let our LOVING Husband reveal Himself, and present Himself through HIS sweet forever Love.

Chapter 15

Andrea

"Give, and it will be given to you.
They will pour into your lap a good measure—
pressed down, shaken together, and running over.
For by your standard of measure will
be measured to you in return."
—Luke 6:38

"I Thought about Cheating to Make Him Suffer"

Andrea, how did your restoration actually begin?

It all started just after returning from a trip that I went on at the end of the year. I went to my sister's and I stayed there for 3 days. It's when I came home that I noticed that my husband was totally different. He didn't talk to me nor would he meet my eyes when we talked. I'm ashamed to say that the moment he went to sleep, I took his phone and went to find out that he was cheating on me. Because he had cheated on me before (with this same person), I made up my mind that I could never trust him again. What's interesting is that I found out here at RMI that Erin says not to trust our husbands, but for an entirely different reason.

Jeremiah 17:5-10 "Thus says the LORD, 'Cursed is the man who trusts in mankind and makes flesh his strength, and whose heart turns away from the LORD. For he will be like a bush in the desert and will not see when prosperity comes, but will live in stony wastes in the wilderness, a land of salt without inhabitant.

"Blessed is the man who trusts in the LORD and whose trust is the LORD. For he will be like a tree planted by the water, that extends its roots by a stream and will not fear when the heat comes; but its leaves will be green, and it will not be anxious in a year of drought nor cease to yield fruit.'"

But at the time I didn't know that. I also didn't know what a mistake it was to confront and ask your husband to choose between us and the Other Woman, because that's what I did and heard the words "I never loved you."

How did God change your situation, Andrea, as you sought Him wholeheartedly?

That's when I started looking for something I could do to get my marriage back and saw a comment that mentioned marriage help online. It was clearly GOD who heard my cries for help, and after this exact moment, He started to transform me. I downloaded the book God restores your marriage and I saw everything I had done to contribute to my situation, causing a crisis and making it worse by doing what everyone says you should do. Each page was like it was written just for me!

Before I found RMI, I just thought about cheating to make him suffer, teaching him a lesson. I thought about finding someone else, someone new and I would use it to get my husband to come back. How foolish and shocking now thinking back to me even considering something so sinful. I'm just so thankful that I started by looking for God with all my heart and then asking Him to change me, change my heart and to teach me how to forgive. This led to how He continues to transform me and give me the gentle and quiet spirit, which He knew I needed to deal with my Earthly Husband and the Other Woman.

What principles, from God's Word (or through our resources), Andrea, did the Lord teach you during this trial?

The principles were: stop all discussions with your husband and forgiveness because that was fundamental to my journey. Letting go was the hardest, but once I let go I grabbed onto my Heavenly Husband with both arms and that's when I really changed and so did my journey and my restoration!

What were the most difficult times that God helped you through, Andrea?

The most difficult was when I started to go through needing an income. I'd not worked prior to this and without a job, things started to lack. Yet this was such a blessing watching the way God supplied all my needs (Phil. 4:19). The moment the Lord became my Husband, He led me to tithe from some money I'd gotten from an accident I was in and that's when the floodgates opened over my life! I was able to pay each of my bills and I became debt-free!!

Luke 6:38—

"Give, and it will be given to you. They will pour into your lap a good measure—pressed down, shaken together, and running over. For by your standard of measure it will be measured to you in return."

Andrea, what was the "turning point" of your restoration?

The turning point was when I let go of everything and came to the point of not wanting my marriage restored. I wanted and needed only Him (after taking the Abundant Life course). That's when my Earthly Husband began contacting me but I wouldn't respond to his texts or calls. Then I finally surrendered to His will and my restoration began.

Tell us HOW it happened, Andrea? Did your husband just walk in the front door? Andrea, did you suspect or could you tell you were close to being restored?

After I replied to his first text, he started to come over every day to have lunch. It began by just being friends again. There were no fights whatsoever. I would mostly nod and listen and if it was something that normally would spark a fight, I was just agreeable (Matt. 5:25). I was shocked just how powerful this one principle is to any relationship!

This entire time we were never intimate, which was fine with me because I didn't need it. I was in such a state of sheer contentment. After this, he asked me to go on a date with him, which was lovely, and later we were intimate again. Before he left he asked me to go to his mother's house over the weekend and while on a walk on their property, he told me he was thinking of returning home. He asked what I thought and I said, "Do whatever makes you happy. I'm really more than fine." He looked hurt but I didn't feel like I had anything else I should say and told God, "I want Your will to be done."

A week later he arrived holding a suitcase and asked if he could stay. I said, "Of course, this is your home." That weekend he asked if I would go to church. I told him I no longer went but that I would go with him. That day he spoke to the pastor after service and in the evening service, he was baptized. I thanked God so much because it was one of my earlier prayers that I stopped praying and told Him I just trusted Him to turn his heart to want to do it and told God that I'd never mention it again nor pray, I would just trust Him.

The other part to complete our restoration is when my Earthly Husband came to me and said he wanted to let me know that he hadn't spoken to the Other Woman for many weeks. He said she kept contacting him, begging him to get together and "just talk" but he said No and blocked her from his phone and social media! Praise be to God because He is God, He alone is faithful and HE fulfilled all He said He would do, every promise I'd believed for He did!

Thank You my God I will never be able to stop thanking You!

Would you recommend any of our resources in particular that helped you, Andrea?

Yes, I recommend God can and will restore your marriage and a wise woman that I read first and continue to read it and will until my last days on earth. I loved the abundant life series too, the encourager, devotionals, psalms and proverbs to stay spiritually fed and spiritually healthy.

Would you be interested in helping encourage other women, Andrea?

Yes

Either way, Andrea, what kind of encouragement would you like to leave women with, in conclusion?

Have faith and believe in God's ability to restore your marriage. Don't you try, instead, focus on Him. Remember He is the God of impossible and what He did for me He will do for you too once He is first in your life!

Chapter 16

Kristin

"Therefore, thus says the LORD,
'If you return, then I will restore you—
Before Me you will stand;
and if you extract the precious from the worthless,
you will become My spokesman.
They for their part may turn to you,
but as for you, you must not turn to them."
—Jer. 15:19

"Accusing Me of Having My Own Lover"

Kristin, how did your restoration actually begin?

In October of last year, my husband left the house due to all the disagreements we had. There were constant fights and we were more distant from each other every day. Even though I was worn out, I knew I still loved my husband a lot. Before he left I asked him to stay, to try again, but he was determined to leave.

From the beginning God led me to fight for the restoration of my marriage, several times, in difficult times. Then one day I was surfing the internet looking for stories of restored marriages, and for people in the same situation as me. As it happened, the Lord led me to the book "How God Can and Will Restore Your Marriage" OMG what a blessing came into my life that day!

I was convinced before that I had been making a lot of mistakes with my husband, but after reading the book I was absolutely sure that I was totally neglecting the Word of God as a wife, that I was very far from the Lord, and that everything that had been happening was God's plan for our lives. By reading through the book and later taking the courses, (which I continue to do by the way), I started to learn to be a wise woman, to seek the Lord more and more and win my husband without words. I had many slips along the way but God was always there beside me to lift me up and guide me. The most difficult thing for me was to learn to let him go, without running after him, but the Lord taught me and helped me to be content.

How did God change your situation, Kristin, as you sought Him wholeheartedly?

The Lord taught me to pray more and more, and I was asking Him to become the wife, mother and woman that He wished me to be. I surrendered myself totally into the hands of God, and He was and still is very much moving in my life. PRAISE GOD, as I know that the work in me and my life is not yet complete. I want to be totally transformed by my God, and above all to be closer to my Heavenly Husband every day. God gave me a meek and quiet spirit, patience to wait, strength to overcome the pain, humility and meekness to keep silent and faith to continue the journey.

What principles, from God's Word (or through our resources), Kristin, did the Lord teach you during this trial?

I committed to reading the Psalms and Proverbs every day, I read the whole RYM book and when I finished, I started again. The same with the courses, I began with Course 1, then 2, then 3, moving into the Abundant Life series. I want to absorb as much as possible. I learned what kind of wife is precious in the eyes of God, how to be submissive to my husband to honor the Lord. Yet the main thing and most precious is to be in the highest place I want to be, "as a bride to the Lord" my Heavenly Husband.

"Therefore, thus says the LORD, 'If you return, then I will restore you—Before Me you will stand; and if you extract the precious from the worthless, you will become My spokesman. They for their part may turn to you, but as for you, you must not turn to them" (Jer. 15:19).

What were the most difficult times that God helped you through, Kristin?

The most difficult moments were when my Earthly Husband told me that he no longer felt anything for me, and then he found out that he was already getting enough from Other Woman, not one, but several. God helped me to overcome each difficulty and gave me the confident heart I needed to continue moving past the battle that was coming against me without being discouraged.

Kristin, what was the "turning point" of your restoration?

A friend and prayer companion I had agreed that when each woman came into my husband's life, that God would act even more powerfully by turning his heart towards me, which is exactly what happened.

Tell us HOW it happened, Kristin? Did your husband just walk in the front door? Kristin, did you suspect or could you tell you were close to being restored?

The woman he was staying with was actually a high school "friend." She came and spent about two weeks with him, then he went back to live with her. At the same time, my husband came back periodically, showing affection towards me, and even expressed jealousy again, accusing me of having my own lover (when in fact I did have a Lover hehehe). That day I had asked the Lord when my husband was going to come back, and I heard God say that He was turning his heart back.

At the time, my husband didn't even come into our house anymore, he was always curt and harsh with me, and just when he appeared to be the most happy, because the Other Woman was with him at his mother's house, it was then that God turned his heart to want only me. One Saturday during a visit with our daughter, he told me he was going to take the Other Woman to the train station that afternoon, that he'd asked her to leave and never contact him again. Then before realizing what was happening, he pulled me close to him and gave me a kiss. A kiss like he'd never given me before. From then on, I just watched the Lord driving everything in our restoration for his return home.

Another request I made to the Lord in my prayers is that before he came back to me he would first turn to the Lord, because he was not yet a Christian. The day after he kissed me, he went to church at the invitation of a friend. He sent me a message telling me and inviting me to the next week's service asking if I would go with him. How wonderful and faithful God is! On the Monday of the following week, my husband was already at our house again, unpacked and he was different! Today I can say what I always dreamed would happen, "As for me and my house we will serve the Lord"!!!

Would you recommend any of our resources in particular that helped you, Kristin?

I recommend everything to be honest with you. I don't believe I've not taken advantage of every one of your resources you have on your sites. Everything is free and it just reminded me of the promise in Isaiah 55:1 "Come, all you who are thirsty, come to the waters; and you who have no money, come, buy and eat! Come, buy wine and milk without money and without cost."

To get started I recommend the book "How God can and will restore your marriage" and purchase in cases of 25 as part of my offering to give to women I hear are having difficulty in their marriages, sharing how it "opened my eyes to the truth and gave me hope." Also "a wise woman" that I will still read. Regardless of where any woman begins, I already know that it is a blessing for each of us as women regardless of our marital status, to take advantage of each of the courses at RMI.

Would you be interested in helping encourage other women, Kristin?

Yes

Either way, Kristin, what kind of encouragement would you like to leave women with, in conclusion?

Seek, trust, and believe in the Lord's promises. All the materials helped me a lot and I am sure it will help many other women, but being in communion with Him and always listening to His voice guiding, loving and strengthening me, was what gave me the courage to continue on my journey. May the Lord be the main purpose of your life, and everything around Him He will work together for your good. Amen!!!! Seek and be blessed by HIM who is beautiful and perfect!!! My Love I fall you in love with You every day!!

Chapter 17

Connie

"I sought the Lord, and He answered me,
And delivered me from all my fears.
They looked to Him and were radiant,
And their faces will never be ashamed."
—Psalms 34:4-5

"I Had So Much Support It Was Destroying Me!"

Connie, how did your restoration actually begin?

It is difficult to specify the moment when everything started to get worse in my relationship with my husband, but personally I believe that after 5 years of marriage and with the birth of our first child, we were little by little having less time with one another. As it became more difficult to find time to be with each other, the frustrated discussions started to increase and our patience began to decrease. We love our children very much and my husband has always been an excellent father but the "we" started to fade and be forgotten behind this new reality that was us being parents.

We were very immature and even though there were always people around us to support us (other Christian couples with more years of believing and married, to whom I continue to honor a lot and to whom I owe a lot of my spiritual growth even though I don't rely on their help any longer), we started looking more and more at each other's defects, feeling misunderstood, tired, unmotivated and when we started looking with the eyes of the flesh then everything began to be compromised.

There are many more reasons that led to this point of exhaustion but there came a time when we were both feeling miserable. I felt that he didn't love me, he didn't value me, and he felt that I didn't honor and respect him. So we started to throw these mistakes in each other's faces. I (stupidly) pressed my husband up against the wall and without being aware of the strength of the words (and above all, unintentionally) I asked him several times if he wanted a divorce! Oh how I regret it!! In addition, in my despair I was becoming more and more contentious. I screamed a lot, I cried, I did not listen to him. I thought he was wrong and that is why when I felt attacked, I attacked with my weapons of the flesh with words that hurt (and much more).

One day he decided he couldn't take it, he said he didn't love me anymore and said that we weren't meant for each other, we were completely incompatible and that together we were going to be nothing but unhappy. My husband suddenly left the house!

At that moment, I completely lost my way. I literally felt that I had been sawn in two—nothing else made sense and I just became apathetic and didn't know what to do. I couldn't handle our children. I couldn't be close to them with the strength and spirit to comfort them and I was like this for more than a few weeks. But God is so good. The same day my husband told me that he didn't love me anymore, my mother (in another country) had a vision I was in trouble, and she began to pray.

How did God change your situation, Connie, as you sought Him wholeheartedly?

The first month was very painful but I was daily in prayer with my mother, with two couples (from our neighborhood who'd asked me if they could pray when they saw my husband moving out) and with some people from our church. Each of these blessed people that God used, never stopped praying for me for my well being, for the boys and for my husband (although they didn't have much faith that he would return that began to unravel my faith). However, without a doubt I had two women who were my great support, two women who gave their lives for me (my mother and a sister from my church). Still, with all that help, I was unable to cope with the spiritual pressure and I went down very easily, because in fact—I had no hope that my husband could or would come back to me.

I knew that God loved me and saw His hand and His supply in my daily life. God was already revealing Himself to me by His Word and in dreams and that was helping me to move forward and getting stronger for the sake of my children but something was still missing—there was no hope that my husband would return home.

I didn't have true hope, on the contrary, the whole drop in my faith was sucked away by the constant comments that everyone said to me. I already had it within me that I would never go through a 2nd marriage, nor did I want a divorce, but around me the comments (even in the Christian community) encouraged me to go on with my life, telling me to move onto another relationship or else I would follow the path of loneliness. Instead, I knew I belonged only to the Lord, and ultimately it was the best thing that's ever happened to me!

However, in the midst of this confusion with my feelings, thoughts and endless barrage of advice I decided it was time to let the Lord work on me. I didn't know my future, I didn't know if my husband was in it or not, but I realized that I certainly needed to be restored as a person and as the Lord was clearly my only Source, it was Him and no one else I wanted to be with, who should I cry out to. I had so much support it was destroying me.

So, in prayer, I told God that I was ready for Him to show me where I had failed, what was my responsibility in this mess. In making this decision, I thought that the way forward would be to look for a Christian counselor/psychologist to help me in this new stage of my life and I also asked a friend to get in touch with a Christian institution who specialized in marriage. However, the waiting list was long and I never heard a response from the counselors again. Thank God for that!!! This was not God's solution or plan! Later I found they never encourage restoration for couples! I had no idea this notion of moving on to find someone new was so predominant in the churches.

God was so faithful that the day after my prayer—I found this ministry—RMI! In fact I had already received an email from a friend some time ago with a link to this ministry, but at that time I was completely indifferent. It took feeling smothered by so much "help" to actually talk to Him about what He wanted for me! On the day that I decided to look at myself—that's when God reminded me of that email from a friend and as soon as I started to read Erin's testimony—my heart felt like it was about to burst! Yes! There is hope, glory to God, there is hope, finally (without a doubt!).

I immediately filled out the Marriage Evaluation Questionnaire and started taking Course 1. Finally I had Hope! What a blessing! What I liked most were all of the verses that Erin presented—the more I read, the more seeds of faith and hope were being planted in my heart, and the joy began to return little by little. Everyone around me could see my excitement for life again!

Furthermore, I immediately felt the confirmation of the Lord, when I read that in this course they were going to focus on "me," on my responsibility, my sin and that was what I had asked God for! I was so grateful because I alone would not know where to start, but God gave me a map, provided by RMI, and I remember perfectly that from that day on—I felt that I had a purpose! I no longer felt lost because the next few months was where I wanted to be!

What principles, from God's Word (or through our resources), Connie, did the Lord teach you during this trial?

The first was to hope. God not only hates divorce, but for Him nothing is impossible and He has the power to incline the hearts of our husbands and ours towards whomever at the appointed time. Another hugely fundamental principle since there were so many who told me the same thing: God does not interfere with free will, so if your husband does not want to be with you, there is nothing that God can do. Those comments killed me the first month and then Erin shared His truth about God turning the heart!

The second principle was to shut up! I meditated and prayed and confessed over and over again the Bible verses that talked about knowing how to keep silent and how a bitter woman ends up being alone (it is so difficult to live with her). I was humiliated (in a good way). With God even correction and teaching became easier to accept. As I was confronted with the truth, I felt shame and regret. But I was able to look at myself and realize how much I needed God to take care of my heart. To change me.

After dealing with this sin, I came to the third principle and the most difficult of all for me. I was available for God to work on me, but I couldn't let my husband go, in fact, I didn't even realize what that meant. I think that practically every week I would pray again to let my husband go and although I wanted to do it and knew how beneficial it would be for me, I confess that it was very difficult. It only happened when I found a new Man. Having a new Man in my life, one I could hold on to, who held onto me, this caused me to stop thinking about my Earthly Husband and soon I no longer wanted my marriage restored.

And finally, the final principle, to give! The Bible says: Give and it will be given to you. After letting go of my church, I started giving my tithe again, but to my true storehouse. My church never prepared me for being a Wise Woman nor did they correctly advise me when my marriage fell apart. So why was I so adamant about attending and giving me tithe to where I'd been starved of the truth?

Also, not just giving financially. RMI taught me I needed to give hope! At first it made me confused. How could I be a blessing to another woman if I myself was feeling so confused and fragile? But God was confirming this in many ways that it was His will that I start to make myself available—me, in my present state—to encourage other women who were facing a marriage crisis. And so, once again, I prayed and asked God how.

It was uncanny because I began having former sisters from the church I once attended asking me to help them or help their friend. Wow, I had the total confirmation that it was God's will. Each of them, almost all the women I spoke to told me after I gave them chapter 1 of RYM that I sent them, they said they felt peace, that they felt so much better after they spoke to me. After I prayed and asked God, He had acted and since then I have become much more radiant because I wanted (and want) to glorify the name of the Lord and it was so good to feel that He was using my life to bless other women!

Lastly, in order to go through this whole restoration process (which is not over yet, it never will be, we go from "glory to glory"), I followed Erin's teachings and made my 3x5 cards with the verses that God was revealing (His promises to me, the verses about my children, my family, protection, fear, faith, in short—everything that God was revealing to me in His Word. In addition to the cards, I meditated on Psalms and Proverbs, I praised the Lord a lot and I submitted many praise reports along my journey.

What were the most difficult times that God helped you through, Connie?

As I said before, my husband was very distant, but even so, we kept in touch and talked about our children. But often it was me contacting him, so the moment I realized I shouldn't call or pressure him to see the boys (again letting him go), I guess it was for two weeks or so I was unreachable. I not only didn't contact him, when he contacted me I waited to reply and for about a week I stopped replying altogether. It was only after God confirmed to my mother that it was time to send him a message and said what I should write and one of the things God said to write is that I loved him (I think that this message was the last blow for the wall of hate to fall completely). I obeyed what I sensed was God and my husband responded in a way he had never done before. He asked for my forgiveness. He thanked me for my understanding of what he'd done and said he wanted to talk to me about everything that was going on. We didn't get together at that time because I had one more test to go through.

One day, I received a letter (which I shouldn't have received, since my husband had given me the address of his new home) from his job, but I didn't realize that the letter was for him, I really thought it was for me (I believe that God didn't allow me to notice at first). When I opened it and realized what it was (by general lines) when I read the first lines, I sensed God telling me to stop reading it. So I immediately stopped reading though I confess I was tempted to read to the end, but then God gave me wisdom to understand that if I did, it would be violating any remaining trust that my husband might have in me. I was able to say in all honesty that as soon as I realized that the letter was not for me, I didn't read it anymore—and that made all the difference when I told my husband!

When he realized that I had received the letter and that I had not been searching in his privacy, it left him more comfortable with me.

The following week we agreed to have dinner here, at home, and after dinner, lunch and after another lunch, the long-awaited conversation happened at the end of the day (after the boys went to sleep). My husband ended up confessing that it didn't make sense to be separated and that this situation that he was going through at work only made him think about us even more and that he would like to come home!

I was not expecting anything at the beginning of the conversation. We started talking about friendship, then dating and finally reconciliation— it was all so fast! I was very happy, but it took me a full two weeks to write this testimony because the change I was waiting for did not happen. It's entirely the enemy who convinced me that what happened was not restoration. But now I know that this is a lie, it is played by the enemy to make us slip in our judgment.

I publicly apologize to God for looking again at the flesh. "Help me, Lord, to stand firm in Your promises and to present a meek and peaceful spirit that pleases You (1 Peter 3:1-7). I want to glorify Your name by loving as You love, forgiving as You forgive, expecting the best from others as You want for us—hope in a love that believes in everything, suffers everything, waits for everything, endures everything! (1 Cor. 13).

For all this, forgive me, RMI, for not having written this before and now I see, I understand that, in fact, the restoration continues. God in His faithfulness has already restored my marriage—HE brought my husband home, He saved my children, me and my husband from living apart. God knows everything, He does everything and I know that He has something new for us every day as we, as a family, continue our restoration journey with Him!! Thank you my Lord!!! Thank you so much for bringing my husband and father of my children back to his home. Thank you my Beloved, how grateful I am, how I love You, how faithful You are!!

Would you recommend any of our resources in particular that helped you, Connie?

All courses! The videos and all that I mentioned above.

Would you be interested in helping encourage other women, Connie?

Yes. My ministry encouraging women will always be part of my life!

Either way, Connie, what kind of encouragement would you like to leave women with, in conclusion?

TRUST HIM. Follow the well laid out plans He revealed to Erin and what this ministry gives freely. Freely give to other women if you want to see restoration in your life and family!

Chapter 18

Hanalen

"Commit your way to the Lord;
trust in Him and He will do this."
—Psalm 37:5

"Back Home a Whole Month Earlier
Thanks to Pandemic"

Hanalen, how did your Restoration Journey actually begin?

First of all, this testimony is a bit delayed, and I want to apologize to
My Love, my HH "Heavenly Husband," for not sharing sooner the
amazing things He has done in my life. All the glory and praise is for
Him!

My journey, unbeknownst to me, began shortly after I met my EH
"earthly husband" about 12 years ago. You see, he was married but
separated, and I was a young girl, who claimed to know God, but went
about it all the wrong way. I entered a relationship with my EH,
knowing he was still legally married (he eventually divorced) but let
me tell you, the troubles in our relationship started early on. Now that
I look back, I knew it was my HH, trying to get a hold of me. In His
greatness. He somehow allowed our relationship to progress, but then I
soon sought my EH above all things. Throughout our entire
relationship, my HH placed many trials in my path to try to get my
attention, to show me that how I was living was wrong, but being
contentious, a know-it-all, and thinking that I had, and would continue
to have, everything under control, God really had to step in.

The first real trial was after my EH and I had married. Just to point out,
we got married when I was 5 months pregnant with our only daughter,
which I knew in my heart was not the way God had wanted things. But
I knew He would forgive me because we did eventually wed. We had
planned a second wedding, 2 years after our initial wedding, to be wed
in the church, our big catholic wedding. A few months before our

wedding, my EH and I had a spat, where I lied to him about something I thought was minor. But little did I know, it was major to my EH. He decided to leave me. He moved out, and refused to have anything to do with me.

Had I been smart, I would have seen the signs then, that God was trying to warn me that the way I was living was going to cause us to crash and burn. I begged my EH to forgive me, to take me back, that I would change my ways. He decided to come back home, and give it another try. I changed, but only for a few months, then I went back to my controlling, and contentious ways. I was the one who wore the pants in our relationship, and I never gave my EH his place as head of our family and home. During this time, I had gone back to school, which really took a toll on our marriage, but my EH was really supportive, and I had high hopes that once I was done, I would go back to focus on us as a couple. Well, sad to say, that wasn't how it ended up. Once I finished school, I started working and continued to neglect my marriage and my home. I became consumed with all of these "great things" that I had become and how accomplished I felt, that I completely missed all of the signs my EH was giving me, and soon he became involved with a coworker, and she became the OW "other woman."

It took about 8 months before God finally had had enough with me and opened my eyes to the relationship that my EH and the OW had been having. To say my life came to a screeching and grinding halt, is an understatement. I confronted my EH, and he didn't deny anything. He said he was tired of the person I'd become, and he had finally found someone who appreciated him the way he felt I should have appreciated him our entire relationship. I started bawling, and begged him again for another chance, for another try at proving to him that I could be exactly what he needed. At first, he refused, but eventually he gave in, and agreed to give it one more try.

This is where the enemy really turned up the fire, and I turned into the worst version of myself. Even I couldn't believe it. I was so consumed with where my EH was, what he was doing, who he was doing it with. I would check phone records, bank accounts, locations. I became unbearable! No one in their right mind would want to be with someone like that! I was also driving myself to the ground. I couldn't eat, I wouldn't sleep. I felt I couldn't trust my EH anymore. My anxiety was so bad, that I would physically make myself sick.

The breaking point was one Friday night about a month after I had found out about the OW. My EH and I attended a concert, we had both been drinking, but I caught him on his phone and saw that he was texting the OW. I started acting like a maniac, and asked my EH how he could still be doing this to me, after everything we'd been through! Well, that was the straw that broke the camel's back for my EH. He sent me home alone, and the next day, he said he could no longer see this marriage working, and he asked me to leave our home. This was the lowest point of my life, everything that I had was gone, in an instant. My biggest mistake was telling all my close family and friends about my situation. But even as I did so, my HH was already working on my heart, because I quickly recognized that I had no one to blame but myself.

How did God change your situation, Hanalen, as you sought Him wholeheartedly?

I did a lot of crying. There were days where I felt I could no longer go on. I still had to continue going to work, and it took every ounce of me to not just quit my job and my life, and curl up into a ball and never face anyone again.

The first few weeks were very difficult because we separated the week before Thanksgiving, so all of the holidays were upon us, including my EH birthday.

What kept me going in the beginning was my daughter, she still needed her mom to be there for her. But soon after, my mother, who actually has experienced a restored marriage herself, sent me a Youtube video, which was about a woman who had been believing God for her marriage and had experienced a restored marriage. Before this, I had little to no hope that God could help me out of the mess that I had made of my life. But something in this video, in the testimony, gave me the faith and strength I needed. It was through a website connected to the video that I stumbled upon the RYM book, but in Spanish. I started reading it immediately, and although I understand Spanish fairly well, I wanted it in English. I tried to go back to the original website, but couldn't seem to find it. Then I came across RMI, and found the RYM book in English. I found Hopeatlast.com, and knew that it really was divine intervention.

It had been about 2 months since our initial separation, and I tried to do everything in the flesh to get my EH to take me back, but to no avail. This was God Himself telling me to stop, that I couldn't do it on my own, that I needed to leave it all to Him and He would repair not only my marriage but me. I couldn't believe how the scales fell from my eyes. I knew that the ways and principles sounded crazy, but what else would I have to lose? I had lost it all, in my eyes already. Little did I know, I was about to gain the best of all, an intimate relationship with my HH, my Love.

What principles, from God's Word (or through our resources), Hanalen, did the Lord teach you during this trial?

The principles that really hit close to home were to have a gentle and quiet spirit, the principle of letting go, won without a word. Letting go was probably the hardest one for me to put into practice. I was so used to always talking and texting my EH, that I was thinking it would be impossible. But my HH helped me along the way. My EH also helped by cutting me off, and asking me not to contact him anymore. I also got all the WOTT books, the Encouraging videos, and started the online courses, and I devoured them all within a matter of weeks. The WOTT books were really what helped to keep my hope alive because my situation seemed so bleak and impossible. My EH continued to remind me that we were not going to get back together, but my HH sustained me through it all.

What were the most difficult times that God helped you through, Hanalen?

The most difficult times were when my EH would flat out reject me and tell me we would never get back together. He would also still want to be intimate with me, and I wouldn't object (since we were separated but not divorced), but then afterward, he would act like I was nothing to him.

Also, every time I tried to take matters into my own hands, and tried to do things in the flesh, and it would only cause things to be worse between my EH and me. Then when the Hate Wall finally came down, my EH would tell me about how he left the OW, but had started seeing a new OW. This almost broke me all over again, but even then, I would sit across from my EH as he poured his heart out and I would just pray to my HH to help me and give me peace and love—to be able to forgive my EH and to love him unconditionally.

There were also times when my EH mentioned filing for divorce, and I had the opportunity to finally tell him that I was a horrible wife, and repented for all of my contentious ways, and told my EH that I wouldn't want to get a divorce, but if that is what he wanted, then I wouldn't stand in his way. Praise God, it never came up again! But even through all of these trials, my HH never left my side. He was always there to remind me that I was enough in His eyes, that He loved me as His bride, and that I was worthy. He was slowly becoming all I wanted and all I needed.

Hanalen, what was the "turning point" of your restoration?

The turning point came when I finally let go of my EH. He had told me not to contact him, and if I did, that he wouldn't respond. So I did as he wished, and also to finally submit to my HH in letting go of my EH and focusing solely on my HH. It was about 2 weeks, when I was finally feeling a peace in my heart that I hadn't experienced before. I had suddenly reached a point where I was okay not being in contact with my EH. I no longer wished to text him, or reach out to him. I was looking more and more forward to spending time with my HH.

I had quite a commute to work, so I began to use this time for prayer and worship. I started to create a playlist of "love songs" that I would sing to my HH. I would have my quiet time to just hang out and talk about my day with My Love. This became such an experience for me, that when I didn't have this time with Him, I felt something was missing. Just as Erin and all the people at RMI say, when you fully let go, that's when my HH decided it was time to start turning the tides (I just never expected it to be so soon).

Shortly after, my EH came over to my sister's house where I had been staying, and we went out together as a family to buy things for my daughter because she was going to start T-ball. When we got back, my EH dropped me off, and then asked if he could use the restroom. When he came out, he told me that he didn't know what had happened, or what made his heart change, but that we had gone from never wanting to get back together, to almost certainly getting back together. He then kissed me, and said there were a lot of things we needed to talk about, but that we would figure it out. I went inside the house, and fell to my knees and started praising my HH, because no one else deserved the glory for that miracle. Only my Heavenly Husband could have done the impossible like He had just done by turning my EH's heart. This helped to completely tear down any hate wall, and opened up communication between my EH and me.

Tell us HOW it happened, Hanalen? Did your husband just walk in the front door?

After that day, my EH and I started to communicate more frequently. He started asking me over to hang out, we would spend time together as a family, he would ask me to spend the night. He also started telling me again that he loved me.

Whenever he spoke about us, he spoke in future terms. Then about a month or so passed, and he started saying that he was preparing to have me come home again. That he had a certain day in April that he had in mind, but that it wasn't an "if" I was coming back, but a "when." He had stopped mentioning the OW, and I never asked, because just as the principles in RYM say, "love believes all things." So, I never questioned him about anything. That proves the great work that my HH had done in me, because the old me would have never been able to keep quiet, I would have blown a fuse, I would have wanted to know every detail. But my Heavenly Husband had changed my heart, He'd given me peace beyond understanding, and I knew that I was to love my EH unconditionally.

But just as things had started progressing with my EH, the enemy came and tried to break me. I was getting a lot of pressure from my sister and her husband, who I was staying with during my separation, to figure out what I was going to do because I couldn't live with them forever. I tried to explain that I was waiting on my HH, because I knew He had a plan for me. You see, my sister knew about my journey with my HH, and RMI, and I even got her the RYM book, but the pressure was coming from her husband, who didn't understand, and wanted me to find my own place and have my EH provide it for me. While the pressure at home was mounting, I had been praying to my HH to restore my marriage by my daughter's birthday.

I had placed this desire in my heart, and didn't mention it again. A few more weeks go by, and word starts spreading about the COVID 19 pandemic. Things are starting to get worse, businesses are starting to close, schools are closing and my sister and her husband tell me that I need to either keep my daughter with me indefinitely (because of what's going on and not have her go back and forth between my EH and I) or I would need to find somewhere else to stay. Even with the mounting pressure, I was still at peace because I knew that no matter what, my Heavenly Husband would take care of me.

It was a Tuesday in March when I was laid off from work, due to the severity of the pandemic, and that same day my EH texted me to have lunch with him. On my drive there, I was SG and prayed that I have peace in my heart, that my HH would give me all the right words to say, and I would not say too much. Once I met up with my EH, he told me that my brother-in-law had texted him pretty much that he needed to step up and provide for my daughter and me because he was tired of doing so! At first, I was stunned, because I could tell my EH was upset and angry. I apologized, and made it clear that I would figure it all out on my own, and that he didn't have to worry. That's when I noticed his demeanor change. He started telling me that he thinks this is a sign that he should have me come back home, that he loved me, and he wanted to work things out. He asked me to forgive him for the things he'd done. He also told me that he wanted me back home, but wasn't quite ready to leave the OW. I was happy and broken all at the same time. I agreed to return home.

On my way to my sister's house, I started crying out for my HH, asking him if this was what He wanted for me, if I had made the right decision in choosing to move back, and at that very moment, a freight truck drove in front of me with a Psalm written on the back of it. It was Psalm 37:5 "Commit your way to the Lord; trust in Him and He will do this." If there was ever a sign more clear than this, this would be it.

I went home, and informed my sister and her husband that I would be moving back home. My sister was thrilled, because she was aware of the journey I had been on, and I'm sure my brother-in-law was just relieved. Another important thing to note, is that the day my EH asked me back home was a whole month earlier than I had asked my Heavenly Husband to return home! Pray and believe, ask and you shall receive! And although my marriage has been restored, but not entirely healed (because there is still the OW), I have faith that my Heavenly Husband will bring all things to completion. He will remain true to His promises, as long as I continue to put Him first in my life.

I look forward to the day that I write my praise report that My Heavenly Husband has completed His good work. In the meantime, I will continue to grow closer to my HH. How could I ever not have Him first? He has changed me far beyond what I could have ever imagined. He has provided for me, and loved me as only a REAL husband can. I will forever love and praise Him all the days of my life. He has come to give me a much greater life, more abundant than I could have ever imagined. PTL!!!

Hanalen, did you suspect or could you tell you were close to being restored?

I only suspected it because my EH kept saying that he was certain he would have me home soon. But no, I didn't expect it to be so fast. Our Heavenly Husband works like that though, He changes things in an instant. I was also thinking that maybe it would happen soon because all of a sudden, things started to get worse. I was being pressured to leave, the pandemic was getting worse, I was on the verge of losing my job. Just as Erin says, when the trials start to get more intense, it means that you're close.

Would you recommend any of our resources in particular that helped you?

I would recommend them all! I would definitely recommend the "Restore Your Marriage" book, even now I still continue to read it, and remind myself of the principles. Definitely the online courses; journaling really helped me to create a more intimate relationship with my HH. All of the WOTT books, they are what gave me the strength and courage to keep pushing forward when all hope seemed lost. The Encourager, Daily Devotionals, Psalms & Proverbs, Questions and Answers. All of it was my fuel, every single one of those things increased my faith in my HH that He could do the impossible not just for me, but for anyone in my situation.

Hanalen, did God give you any special promises you'd like to pass on to women reading your Testimony?

"Commit your way to the Lord; trust in Him and He will do this:" Psalm 37:5 NIV

"For my thoughts are not your thoughts, nor are your ways My ways, says the Lord." Isaiah 55:8

"For I know the plans I have for you," declares the Lord, "plans to prosper you and not to harm you, plans to give you hope and a future." Jeremiah 29:11

"I am confident of this, that the One who began a good work among you, will bring it to completion by the day of Jesus Christ." Phillipians 1:6

"Looking at them, Jesus said, "With people it is impossible, but not with God; for all things are possible with God." Mark 10:27

"Wives, be subject to your own husbands, as is fitting to the Lord" Col. 3:18.

"We know that God causes all things to work together for good to those who love God, to those who are called according to His purpose" Rom. 8:28.

And so many more!

Would you be interested in helping encourage other women, Hanalen?

Yes! Of Course!

Either way, Hanalen, what kind of encouragement would you like to leave women with, in conclusion?

Our Heavenly Husband is here to change our lives for the better. There is no one on this planet who will love you, provide for you, comfort you, lift you up like He will. Give your troubles and struggles to Him, even your marriage, because only He can heal us and our marriages. I encourage you to seek God in all things, and watch how your life becomes transformed into something far greater than you can ever imagine!

Hanalen, you submitted a praise report a few weeks after restoration, what did He do for you?

I would like to start by thanking My Love, my HH for continuing to work in my life every single day, even when I feel unworthy and when I've made mistakes. He does not leave us or abandon us, He loves us like a real Husband would!

This week I've been feeling like the enemy has been coming at me hard, I've had so many feelings of doubt, and inadequacy, thinking that My Love has forgotten about me and man I couldn't have been more wrong. Once I really sat down and spoke to my HH, He gave me a word. It was so clear, that it came to me 3 different times in just one week. It was 2 Peter 3:9 "The Lord is not slow in keeping his promise, as some understand slowness. Instead he is patient with you, not wanting anyone to perish, but everyone to come to repentance."

It made me realize that the thoughts that I was allowing to consume me, were against His principles, the very principles that allowed me to receive my restoration. He placed in my heart the need to ask for His forgiveness, for wanting to again do things in the flesh, and I'm so thankful for His word. Don't give up ladies, and when you're feeling attacked, don't think it's because Our Beloved has left your side, on the contrary, He is always there, comforting us, loving us. Allow your heart to experience His love. And don't ever forget that we should take our troubles to Him, and no one else.

Pray with me: My Love, help me to see how you're using all the enemy meant for evil for your good. Remind me that your ways are not our ways, and that we must be patient, just as you are patient in us. Forgive me when I fall short, and strengthen me to continue on this journey. I know your word will not come back void, and we must delight and praise you always! Amen!

Chapter 19

Kayla

"Older Women…encourage the young women
to love their husbands, to love their children,
to be sensible, pure, workers at home, kind,
being subject to their own husbands, so that
the word of God will not be dishonored."
—Titus 2:3-5

"I was in Love! I Lived in a Bubble"

Kayla, how did your Restoration Journey actually begin?

I come from a family of 10 daughters. We didn't have any biological brothers, so later my parents adopted a boy. Before that, imagine a house with 11 females and one male (my father). My mother didn't have time for us and didn't teach us how to be wives. When I got married I had my mother who I mirrored. Even though I was one of the calmest, I was still influenced by her example, she liked to argue, to be right, and was contentious and quarrelsome, which I mimicked becoming my "qualities" as well.

I met my husband through my mother-in-law. After we spent just a short time together, we got married. We went to church and my husband accepted Him as his Lord and Savior and started to work in ministry. Following my mother's example, who was always at home and always left my father alone, I did the same. My husband played sports and I didn't— I didn't follow anything he did, I just wanted to work and take care of the house as I learned.

Over time we had a daughter and then my time with my EH was less than nothing. When he left the Lord's work, then I started a ministry in the church. We lived our lives differently, separately. Many times he warned me that it's a mistake to live our lives like this. He made several attempts to approach me, but I didn't care. To me, my marriage was great. It was then that he distanced himself. Once a man who was very affectionate became distant, that didn't make sense, until one day when I fiddled with the computer, unintentionally discovering many things I wish to God I hadn't seen!

Enraged, I fought, said he was going to leave because I didn't trust him. Full of suspicions and more jealousy, I considered kicking him out. That's when a friend sent me a link to the book (How God can and will restore your marriage). The moment I started reading it I was in shock! I started to see everything I had done and how much I gave my husband to the world and I didn't take care of the family that the Lord gave me.

Then something happened inside me, I saw my mistakes, but my pride wouldn't let me change. I chose to believe I was the victim. As I read, things fell into place inside me, but I still resisted. I kept leaving my EH alone and everything he did that I didn't like, each of his mistakes, I threw in his face. After a while, he didn't care anymore. I wanted to change, but I couldn't. I continued to stay at home and didn't accompany him anywhere when he asked me to come.

How did God change your situation, Kayla, as you sought Him wholeheartedly?

God broke me and started to build me back up with His love. I joined RF, began taking your courses, let go of church, didn't talk about my marriage to anyone anymore and the Lord became my Husband. Shortly after this, I didn't know how to live without Him anymore.

Time passed and even though I read the books, taking the courses, I no longer really had a marriage and that made me suffer a lot, feeling I was a fraud. My EH was almost no longer at home. He was living a life apart from us (me and my daughter). Then one day he said we needed to be separated, and went to live with his mother, while my daughter and I stayed in our home—and my beloved Husband. It was there that I gave myself totally to the Lord...when my EH had given up on us. That's when the Lord became my Husband and took care of me all the time. I worked a lot (early morning until late in the evening) and the commute was grueling. I took 3 buses to get to work but that's when I read the Psalms and Proverbs every day. I began reading through the Bible and made sure to wear dark glasses so no one would see me cry.

I honestly never felt more cared for, more loved, more forgiven and life was beginning to spring up inside me! It was my Beloved who was stirring things inside and comforting me. He began healing me from all childhood wounds, mistakes I'd made during my adolescence, and the guilt of my failed marriage. I started to smile and longed to be with Him. At lunchtime, I would run to eat and enjoy an hour listening and reading the Word. I let everything go and left it in His hands. I was in love! There is no other way to describe it! He provided everything for me and changed my temper. I didn't look for my EH for anything. I thought he might have someone, but I didn't know anything, nor did I care. My Beautiful Husband protected me from everything. I lived in a bubble.

What principles, from God's Word (or through our resources), Kayla, did the Lord teach you during this trial?

Letting go was a struggle at first. I didn't look for him, but I thought about him all the time. But little by little, my HH was transforming me and I just wanted to be with HIM and my daughter, I didn't care much about what my EH did. He lived at my mother-in-law's house that was near our home, so he stopped by our house every day. When he was there, I treated him well, did not argue or ask about when he would return or what he was doing. To be honest, I was anxious for him to leave so I could be with my Beloved. I watch the videos of Erin speaking to me. I learned a lot. When I was downcast, I cried out to the Lord and He answered me, loved me, and filled the emptiness inside me. Things I never learned to be I was now becoming: a wife, a friend, a companion. He was making these things born again in me and the guilt of not having done this in my life faded.

The thought of marriage also faded away. He was all I wanted, needed, and lived for. Then one day I looked at my EH for the first time in ages and I saw his suffering. Something very serious was going on, clearly a battle within him. It was my HH stirring things around inside him too. He approached me, then immediately distanced himself from me at the same time. I no longer suffered, but I was loving my HH so much that I just wanted Him and no other.

What were the most difficult times that God helped you through, Kayla?

The most difficult hours were watching him arrive at dawn because I live in the upstairs apartment of my mother-in-law's house. And when he spent nights away, the enemy taunted me. But my Beloved took care of me at all times and I fell asleep and rested in perfect peace.

Kayla, what was the "turning point" of your restoration?

The turning point was when I found out about an OW. She put a picture of them on her WhatsApp profile and I saw it. I was on the bus and started to cry as she was a close friend. I called him and asked if he would just ask her to take the picture down so people wouldn't see it and it would get back to our daughter. He ignored me, said No, and said he was on her side. I hung up the phone and went home heartbroken for our daughter and our families. He followed me home and told me many things I said I didn't want to hear. But he also said that he loved me and that he only stayed with other women because I was not a companion to him, I always left him alone. He begged me, saying he wanted his family back. I accepted, but inside I knew I just wanted to be alone with my Husband. I cried a lot because he told me about everything he had done for nearly two years (getting involved with her the moment he had left the house seven months prior). So we agreed to talk more during the week, but he also kept in touch with OW.

Tell us HOW it happened, Kayla? Did your husband just walk in the front door? Kayla, did you suspect or could you tell you were close to being restored?

We spent a week talking and on Saturday my EH returned home. He moved all of his things downstairs and the first thing he did was to show me the picture of them was down (glory to God). Today he is happily at home and enjoys being with us. He said he wants to get married in the church (because we were married at a justice of the peace) and has spoken to his pastor. He demanded that I leave the company where I worked and I immediately left without challenging him.

We are starting over. He enrolled me in the gym where he works out and we now enjoy working out together. We went to the circus this week and we are making a lot of plans to do things together, the two of us or as a family. My Lord is beautiful and He, no doubt, performed a miracle on me. A new woman was born again...a woman who smiles, who talks, and who enjoys being with her EH.

My EH doesn't want to talk about the Bible or being my spiritual leader yet. But as I learned at RMI, we must be chaste and respectful so that our husbands, even if disobedient to the Word, are won without a word. I don't know if he's in contact with OW, but I don't worry. It is in the hands of God who has control of all things. "The king's heart is like channels of water in the hand of the Lord; He turns it wherever He wishes." Proverbs 21:1

Would you recommend any of our resources in particular that helped you, Kayla?

The Be Encouraged videos, the book (how God can and will restore her marriage) A Wise Woman helped so much to give me the training I lacked to be the kind of woman God created us all to be. The Daily Encourager, also reading the testimonies to understand what mistakes to avoid and better paths to take in our journey, and especially reading the Bible. Reading through it has become my favorite resource of all!

Would you be interested in helping encourage other women, Kayla?

Yes

Either way, Kayla, what kind of encouragement would you like to leave women with, in conclusion?

Do not give up on yourself or your families. He gave me back the joy of living when I met Him for the first time and then later, once we were in love. God restored my marriage while I fell in love with my HH. He can do all things. It was never about us, nor for what we can do. It's all about Him and everything He can do. He's wonderful!!!

Chapter 20

Brianna

"You will not fear bad news, your heart is
firmly confident in the Lord."
—Psalm 112:7

"Countless Questions, Doubts, Anxiety, and Fear"

Brianna, how did your Restoration Journey actually begin?

My story is long and began 4 years ago when I had a wedding ceremony, a gathering of family and friends at the registry office. Before this, the pastor had spoken to me about his concerns, but due to lack of commitment to God and never understanding about the authorities over me, I did not listen. But afterward, this brought me countless questions, doubts, anxiety, and fear.

I also didn't know if RMI was the right place for me when I first came, for a while I refused to hear the truth and went against the ministry's principles by not being legally married. Realizing that I once again ignored the authority over me and even ignored what I knew was the truth!

It was a long two and a half year journey. I fell, I got up, I fell again, I entered the world, I got tired and I returned. God always rescues me and this ministry has always given me time and space. Praise the Lord for this! God even took my ex to another country for months, there were miles separating us, and it was then that I found out he was with someone else. I saw the family supporting him at the same time while he ignored me and treated me with carelessness. I saw I had suffocated him because I didn't let him go in my heart the way I knew and was taught to.

After two months, I finally stopped chasing after him, calling and texting but my heart still yearned and I did all my RMI courses in search of restoration, just restoration with a man, my focus was not the Lord. This brought me countless more questions, doubts, anxiety, and fear.

How did God change your situation, Brianna, as you sought Him wholeheartedly?

It was through a cousin that God changed the whole situation, This cousin sent me two songs in a conversation, the first opened my eyes about my relationship condition. Regardless of what I lived, everything was undone and what came would be new! It didn't matter what my relationship status was because it was over. I knew the truth and it set me free. The second song talked about looking for God in all things, getting answers. From then on, I started to see the Ministry as a support for my recovery with the Lord! I became discouraged and started to realize that I am the daughter of a King, belonging to a Heavenly Husband. I started to see my value and the lack of value that the world offers. Once I finally understood about obeying what RMI says, I started to become content. My heart was happy with everything that was taught.

What principles, from God's Word (or through our resources), Brianna, did the Lord teach you during this trial?

The principle of letting go was of paramount importance. Both this and the principle of tithing are the ones I advise everyone to read over and over until they get it. Once I settled with RMI the enemy's hold on me was over. I wasn't doubleminded. I started to see God's care for me and as it happened I wanted to shout how glorious it is having Him as the Love of my life and letting go was flowing naturally.

What were the most difficult times that God helped you through, Brianna?

The most difficult times happened when I saw my ex with the OW and his family, even my own family supporting his decision. The times when I heard him talk about future plans which did not include me. It was terrible to imagine that I was no longer part of his life, it hurt a lot. Thankfully those days passed once I found and embraced my true Love.

Brianna, what was the "turning point" of your restoration?

The turning point was when I stopped going out before I even got back to work at RMI. God was already in my heart opening my eyes to countless situations I'd gotten involved in where I was acting like a harlot. As I began to please Him, He rewarded me with so much love and care. I didn't need the world and the things it offered that left me lonely. My eyes were opened and I began to witness how beautifully God took care of me, removed all the pain and fear I felt, and many other things. The more I saw His acting on my behalf, the less I felt like looking for or expecting something from my ex or anyone else. I started to let it go in my heart and this was also a turning point because suddenly I heard my ex was going to visit a Christian friend, soon after my ex started talking to me all the time, I saw him inviting me to countless things.

Tell us HOW it happened, Brianna? Did your husband just walk in the front door? Brianna, did you suspect or could you tell you were close to being restored?

My ex, as I said, never stayed away for long. I have always had contact and we had a close friendship. This, on the one hand, is good but on the other hand, is difficult because without being prepared I made mistakes and prolonged this journey a lot! I can say that he just showed up to talk about our marriage and this time doing it right, in a church before God. I didn't have to say anything, I nodded and agreed as he told me how important it was to do everything right this time.

To get married in the church, he said, was a dream he never had considered but that he began to yearn to see me as a bride, and that it was important that when we got married in the church all the family needed to be present.

Everything came together quite suddenly. Everyone attended and everyone helped with the details. There was an opening at the church when a couple decided to call it off, so I can happily announce I am RESTORED and a married woman. I have been transformed due to my relationship with the Lord and this is worth more than anything! Words I never thought I would say let alone feel so deeply in my heart!

Would you recommend any of our resources in particular that helped you, Brianna?

I advise reading the book How God Can and Will Restore Your Marriage, I advise reading A Wise Woman, especially for women who have not yet legally married, it is especially transformative for us! I also advise the courses and all that the ministry offers with the daily devotional, courses 1 and 2 are transforming. But life-changing is the Abundant life series that cannot be missed.

Would you be interested in helping encourage other women, Brianna?

I will continue doing my courses to prepare for ministering. Yes, I am available to help and I look forward to helping all ministries and people who come here.

Either way, Brianna, what kind of encouragement would you like to leave women with, in conclusion?

I can tell you, everything that is written and said by Erin is based on the Word and "Your Word is the truth from the beginning." (Psalm 119:160) Do not be afraid to give yourself to God, to our Heavenly Husband, it is from Him that all things come. Give yourselves to His promises and begin your day reading of Psalms and Proverbs, so that your heart is filled with them in times of need!

Today, when I am about to fall, my mind thinks "Commit your way to the Lord; trust in him, and he will act." (Psalm 37:5) The verse "You will not fear bad news, your heart is firmly confident in the Lord." (Psalm 112:7)

He also lives in my heart. I would now like to give all the honor and glory to the Lord. This is a journey, mine started by only looking forward to restoration with my ex, and today, it comes down to restoration with my Beloved. It is Him that I want to please, Him I want a relationship with, to build my house on the Rock, to continue growing and be with HIM. Praise the Lord for everything, I love and thank Him for such loving care of me!

Chapter 21

Rebecca

"He sent His word and healed them,
And delivered them from their destructions."
—Psalms 107:20

"Sad Because He was Forced to Kiss Me"

Rebecca, how did your Restoration Journey actually begin?
Hello, Beloved! My story begins 8 years ago when I met my husband. We met when we were very young, he was 19 and I was 14 years old and our relationship was short because at 6 months I went to live with him. Because my mother did not approve, due to the fact that I was very young (and she was not wrong, today being a mother I understand this so well!!). My relationship had always been good, with a few fights, some comings, and goings (short), all in all, things were better than anyone thought it could be.

After four years, when I was 18, I got pregnant with my first daughter, we had become a little distant but this unexpected pregnancy brought us very close. We moved to another city, we went to live outside the busy city, we had a few financial difficulties, but we were always together. After three years we built our house and I became pregnant with my second, a son and that's exactly when it all started, I was 6 months pregnant when we had a fight over money. His cousin's son was having a birthday and I didn't want us to go because we were short on funds, but my EH loves socializing and being with people. So he bought a gift without telling me that we were going, he came home from work and said he would go and take our daughter. I went crazy, a completely contentious woman, and shouted I wouldn't go and he was not allowed to take our daughter. He was very angry with me (and he is naturally calm), but what got worse was when he came back at midnight and wanted to give her a piece of cake and I once again screamed that if he woke her up, I would make such a scene. We went more than a month without speaking to each other and to make it worse, to make my point, I left and stayed at my mother's house for a week that only made everything between us worse.

How did God change your situation, Rebecca, as you sought Him wholeheartedly?

Beloved, the fact is, I was always a bad wife and it was my husband who always tried to make it work, but I always complained, nothing was good enough. I was the foolish woman that Proverbs describes, she is exactly me! I grew up in a Christian home so I knew that I had to seek the restoration of my marriage, that this was God's will. Each day I went to pray, I just cried. I went to the church looking for help and I talked to the pastor who told me to look in faith that things were going to work out, but it wasn't easy. I didn't know what to do.

While gone, my EH went out to party, he ignored me when he got home, he arrived drunk, he didn't even look at me. But I knew I was to blame for all this because I planted seeds to be reaping those fruits. Because it is not enough for you to be an excellent housewife if you are not a wife as the word of God teaches.

What principles, from God's Word (or through our resources), Rebecca, did the Lord teach you during this trial?

I searched for testimonies about restored marriages on the internet and saw comments and testimonies related to HopeAtLast. And as soon as I found the page and filled out the questionnaire, I started the course. At the beginning I did more than one class a day, I was so desperate even though it said to do just one each day.

From day one, I wanted to put the Lord as the priority in my life but I couldn't, I was always crying and sad and desperate to get my husband back. But prayer is an ally of faith. I prayed a lot and prayed each promise I read in the daily encourager in my prayers. I followed everything the courses taught, and I had a relationship with God that really changed my life and behavior. And I understood that all I was going through was for me to meet a powerful God that I did not know and that surprised me every day. My biggest surprise was that many times, even while painful trials were happening, I did not feel anything once I found my HH. My HH, my Lover, gave me the PEACE and so much love my heart could burst.

What were the most difficult times that God helped you through, Rebecca?

There were many moments when I wanted to give up, just leave the house but because God is so good, I never left and He didn't allow him to leave. There were times I thought I couldn't take it. But just feeling His presence, I was overjoyed. Then I got a call from my EH, who said he saw how much I changed but that he didn't love me anymore and that he was going to hopefully still be able to pay our bills, but he was going to rent a room for him to live elsewhere. I didn't despair, because I knew the enemy was furious because I was in such a close relationship with the Lord. So I said "okay" and he was shocked. He told me later he was expecting me to lash out. Beloved, I want to stress something about my relationship with the Lord and why you must be intimately close with Him if you want to experience restoration, first with the Lord, then secondly in your marriage with your husband.

Rebecca, what was the "turning point" of your restoration?

The turning point was gradual, seed by seed I had sown. We started to get closer little by little, we began to be intimate, but he didn't come back to our house to live and I never felt that he wanted to. Then the day came and I went into labor. As we drove to the hospital, I was happy and excited to see my baby, but at the same time, I was sad because my EH was there as the father, not as my husband. When our son was born, the nurse asked my EH to kiss me, which was both embarrassing and extremely sad because he was forced to kiss me.

At home, we were still at odds but I was persevering. More and more I realized I had something so much better than any earthly relationship, which is the love of the Lord as my HH, who embraced me and took care of me as my EH never did or ever could. So I changed my prayers for God to save him, and if it wasn't His will for us to be together, so be it. I was tired of the whole situation, of trying and I just gave up. I trusted the Lord and knew He would do what was best for me and our family. And that was what TURNED everything—because when we put the Lord first, and give up so God can restore, it makes all the difference in the world!

Tell us HOW it happened, Rebecca? Did your husband just walk in the front door? Rebecca, did you suspect or could you tell you were close to being restored?

My EH began coming to sleep at home and then came back to sleeping in our bed, each time, we were slowly getting closer. A month later it was my birthday but he did not remember. Normally I would have been devastated, but I said nothing. He apologized afterward but because he was late to work nothing more was said.

I thought that was God showing me that our marriage was not His perfect plan for me.

A week later, he got into bed to go to sleep and I went to take a bath. When I got out of the bath my husband was sitting on the bed and asked me to sit next to him, and FINALLY said he wanted us! He wanted to be married to me more than anything. Not only is my marriage restored but now I have my LOVING HEAVENLY HUSBAND!

As I've read in so many testimonies, a husband's return is both complicated and sensitive, which is why we have to trust God to complete everything while we remain focused on our HH. This keeps us doing our courses and continuing to apply everything we learn here. God is acting and strengthening my marriage every day. It's been six months and He continues to amaze me every day!

Would you recommend any of our resources in particular that helped you, Rebecca?

Girls read and reread HOW GOD CAN AND WILL RESTORE YOUR MARRIAGE, begin with the daily devotionals, take the courses, read testimonies, and especially the Bible. You must strengthen yourself in the Lord, let Him talk while you listen, and OBEY. Be sure to enjoy this time to be intimate with Him, let His Word wash over and heal you!!!

Would you be interested in helping encourage other women, Rebecca?

YES, if you need my help I'm here!

Either way, Rebecca, what kind of encouragement would you like to leave women with, in conclusion?

Your marriage will be restored if you allow God to do it. Yes, God is allowing you to go through this desert so that you finally get to know it's really and truly about being His bride so that you can be loved by Him and have PEACE! Be patient, it is very worthwhile to wait on the Lord. Cry only for Him and to Him. Look to Him and be radiant. Turn it over to God, give everything to Him

Chapter 22

Paulina

"Those who sow in tears shall
harvest with joyful shouting."
—Psalm 126:5

"Happy to be Separated from 'That Man'"

Paulina, how did your restoration actually begin?

First of all, I want to thank you all for the opportunity that God has given me to be redeemed again by His love! I thank everyone in this ministry that welcomed me and taught me that I should only have God as my refuge and look for my answers from Him alone!

It all started 17 years ago, we married as a lot of young people do and we had high hopes for our perfect marriage. Since I was never an easy going person, I went into my marriage being full of myself, as I was aggressive, spoiled, arrogant, a complete Pharisee! I thought I was the ruler of everything and because of that, my attitude was pushing my husband away from me and into the sins of the flesh. I did just like Samson played with sin.

In the third year of my marriage, I got involved with a man, it was a very painful experience when my husband discovered what was going on but he decided to forgive me. As time passed my unhappiness only increased, I did what I wanted, I was not submissive. Even after being forgiven, I continued to flirt with 2 more guys, which ended up being the final straw. So was social media that you all explain is so dangerous.

On Facebook, a man sent me a reply and was pretty much asking me to be with him. My husband discovered the messages and our marriage ended. I was foolishly a bit glad it happened, we hardly spoke to each other anymore, our intimacy ended, understanding was gone, and I was just thinking how happy I was to be separated from "that man."

How did God change your situation, Paulina, as you sought Him wholeheartedly?

Soon after reality hit. My husband left, packed everything telling me that we didn't have any more to give and that he didn't love me anymore. I didn't expect this. I could see in his eyes how angry he was at me. Within my arrogance, I thought he would never leave me and told myself that soon he'd return home. He did and trying to keep him, I stopped the pill and soon I became pregnant with our third child.

At first, I thought "now he'll be ready to come back home where he belongs" but all I saw and heard was more hurtful and the anger he had was more intense and he moved further away. In May, my life changed when I found the RMI site. I was desperate for restoration and I was looking for a solution day and night for my husband to return.

From the moment I started to take the course, my focus was no longer only on my husband and my quest to get him back. I spent the last few months of my pregnancy falling in love with my Beloved and soon He was my Heavenly Husband. His love was transforming me and right away my husband started to notice some small changes, that he acknowledged but couldn't believe were true.

I was learning how I was wrong when I destroyed my family like a fool. So my first step was to ask my husband for forgiveness. I wrote everything I needed to confess to him and said everything that was heavy on my heart. Then, I started to rebuild a relationship with my children.

I sought God, I became very thirsty for His Word and He consoled me while I was in great emotional pain. As my pregnancy progressed, my husband only moved farther away. God used it for good as it was just me and my HH alone.

What principles, from God's Word (or through our resources), Paulina, did the Lord teach you during this trial?

The main and most difficult principle to apply was to let go. Whenever I decided I'd let go, I ended up going back with my obsession to do SOMETHING to get him back, which ultimately delayed the restoration of my marriage. I wanted my will and ended up giving up after being worn out. Going around and around with this one principle I had trouble grasping.

Another principle that I found difficult was to maintain an intimacy with my husband, because he always made it very clear to me that I was not supposed to have hope because the only feeling he had for me was for this one thing. When I heard this from him it was as if someone was putting a knife in my chest. At those moments, I just continued asking the Lord to be with me so that I could be a beautiful and loving wife to my husband. In the end, God rewarded my obedience.

What were the most difficult times that God helped you through, Paulina?

Every period of the journey was difficult. I felt pain every day and there were days when the pain was so intense that I couldn't get out of bed.

Things finally came to a conclusion when I found out that he was with an OW, my world collapsed, I couldn't believe he was with OW and I almost went crazy. During this period I was about 7 months pregnant, the news was so overwhelming that I left home and ended up at my aunt's house. That's where God spoke to me. He said He would be with me, that the restoration was happening and that He was the One fighting for me. Even though I trusted the promises from the Lord, I had many moments of doubts and questions. Yet His love, as always, came through!

Paulina, what was the "turning point" of your restoration?

The turning point was when I understood that if I didn't get out of the way, let my husband go that God would not be able to do anything. Then he goes on accepting everything that was even proposed for divorce.

Tell us HOW it happened, Paulina? Did your husband just walk in the front door? Paulina, did you suspect or could you tell you were close to being restored?

A month before the scheduled court date for our divorce hearing, God had placed it in my heart to do a Daniel's fast for 21 days. While at my prenatal appointment, that was on the day of the hearing, He confirmed it was Him calling me to fast when my doctor told me my blood pressure was way down and I was in the best condition I'd ever been in during any of my pregnancies! I knew this was God telling me He was guiding me and to trust Him.

Before I could get to the court for the hearing, I got a call from my husband that it had been rescheduled for 14 days later. Throughout this process, it was clear that my husband's anger towards me was in no way diminishing. He despised me and always reminded me that I was an adulteress (reminding me of how I'd been unfaithful in our marriage). This only made me intensify my trust in Him because only God could restore what I'd destroyed so thoroughly!

Before the rescheduled divorce hearing, our son was born and the huge transformation began. It was clear to see God was changing my husband, turning his heart. When I looked at him I could see he no longer hated me and felt much closer.

On the rescheduled court hearing, as we sat waiting outside, we talked for almost 3 hours waiting for our hearing to start. During the conversation he asked me if I had one more chance what would I do?? I knew God had orchestrated everything. Rather than divorce, God restored my marriage!

We left the courthouse together, and after he dropped me home, he arrived back the next morning and said that he wanted to talk to me. He asked me to find a sitter so the two of us could have dinner out. During our dinner, he said he was coming home, that it ended with OW weeks earlier, and that he was going to give us another chance. It wasn't how I dreamed it would be but it was the perfect way God planned it and that's why it was better than I'd ever dreamed.

Would you recommend any of our resources in particular that helped you, Paulina?

Yes, in addition to the courses it was the praise reports that were fundamental pieces to keeping me encouraged. I recommend How God can and will restore your marriage and wise woman to build your life on.

Would you be interested in helping encourage other women, Paulina?

Yes

Either way, Paulina, what kind of encouragement would you like to leave women with, in conclusion?

Don't give up, don't get discouraged, don't stop believing in God's promises. Get involved with God, become intimate with your HH. Don't worry about tomorrow, but be focused on being in love with your HH. You must let Him fight for your marriage while you rest in Him. Your journey is very worthwhile even going through a lot of pain. If God did this miracle in my life as an adulteress just imagine all He will also do in your life. Remember, there is nothing impossible for God.

Immerse yourself in the Word of God and live His promises as it is in Isaiah 30:18. God will always do what is best for us. Please remember when you're weary that GOD restored my hopeless marriage, which I totally destroyed, was without hope and God made everything new, transforming me and our marriage. I know He will surely do the same for you and your marriage too.

These were some verses that helped me a lot in difficult times.

John 15:7

Proverbs 4:23 and 25

Psalm 71:20

Psalm 126:5 and 6

Jeremiah 15:21

Proverb 21:1

Matthew 19:26

Love God with all your heart and don't give up!!

Chapter 23

Alana

"Those who go out weeping,
carrying seed to sow,
Will return with songs of joy,
carrying sheaves with them."
—Psalms 126:6

"The Day the Ground Opened Up and Swallowed Me"

Alana, how did your Restoration Journey actually begin?

My Restoration Journey, I believe, started on the day that my EH (earthly husband) said he did not want our marriage anymore. That was 8 months ago and that day the ground opened up and swallowed me. However, during the journey I was being shaped by my Beloved and He was showing me that this situation started long before that. With the time I spent with Him, my Beloved was showing me moments, situations and attitudes that culminated in the "death" of my marriage. That was one of the words my EH (earthly husband) used to describe the situation, he said that our marriage had died.

What actually happened was that our marriage that had turned into a coldness really died and my Beloved began resurrecting it into a whole new marriage. Describing things a bit better, it happened like this: one morning my husband left home without telling me. We had been distant and cold with each other for some time. He was working 2 jobs and I also worked and had become a spiteful and quarrelsome person. When I woke up I called him and was super angry demanding an explanation, he yelled at me and said he didn't want to be married anymore. From then on, things only got worse. I contacted our pastor and I told him, so he went to talk to my husband and he was offended. Huge mistake! In the beginning, my EH (earthly husband) stayed at home sleeping on the couch and we even had intimacy on occasion. However, after about a month, because I hadn't changed, he decided to leave the house. Thanks to my Beloved's compassion, in the first week I searched the internet for marriage restoration and found your book that I read in a few days. So when he left the house I was already being restored in my soul by my Beloved so I was able to let him go with no fights or demands.

How did God change your situation, Alana, as you sought Him wholeheartedly?

From the first moment, I had access to the book and courses the scales that were in my eyes fell, all of the pride and arrogance from self-love. I saw who I really was and I didn't like the person I saw. My Beloved showed me each day how much I needed to change. I remember nights that I spent crying and asking Him to change me, begging Him to take all the hardness out of my heart. I learned with your courses and with my HH (Heavenly Husband) the principles of the Word and I became the woman who is precious in the eyes of God with a gentle and quiet spirit. Time passed and the more I searched for my Heavenly Husband the more my EH (earthly husband) approached and reached out to me. During this journey, he and I have never lost touch that not all brides are blessed with. We have a 5-year-old son so to encourage his dad to come more, I always left when my EH (earthly husband) came to our home. I will never forget the generosity of my Beloved during the months we were only two. He provided everything for me and in abundance as He said He would. His love turned me into a new person that I believed had never happened after becoming Christian more than 15 years ago. For I believed that I already knew Him, but He showed me that I was not even close to meeting Him. That is why I praise and thank you for this journey, for this ministry, because it made me really know Him and have a true relationship with Him!

What principles, from God's Word (or through our resources), Alana, did the Lord teach you during this trial?

There were so many principles that I was able to learn and I am very grateful to my Beloved and to this ministry for learning each one of them, but of course, there were some that changed me more than others. One of the things that most impressed me was the principle of being silent and winning others without words, but also of being quiet in order to be discreet about a situation that everyone these days just blurts out without a thought of the consequences. I was impressed by how much this really works! When I stopped talking about the situation, my flesh stopped being fed and I noticed that whenever I slipped and talked about it, my flesh emerged and feelings of pain, anger and bitterness came pouring back. Keeping silent, together with the principle of fasting, gave me a new perspective on the whole situation. It made me see the will of my Beloved before each trial.

Another essential principle was letting go and I could see that it has many phases, from letting it go in the physical, then letting go by not even thinking about the other person or marriage restoration. The final letting go was in the heart. The best thing about learning to let go is that in the same measure that we let our EH (earthly husband) go, the more of our HH (Heavenly Husband) we get and then we feel loved, valued and desired again! That is totally different from how we felt when we were seeking and longing for our EH (earthly husband). And that is when the real joy and the joy of having the Lord as our Heavenly Husband really takes hold and changes us!

What were the most difficult times that God helped you through, Alana?

There were many situations that felt like my insides were a burning fiery furnace but He was always there with me. I remember that the few times that EH (earthly husband) tried to come back and a few days later he left again were terrible moments. At first I felt all the pain of rejection again, but over time these situations became less and less impactful and every time His Love remade me and made me better and more refined just as gold is refined by fire.

The last ordeal of this type was when my EH (earthly husband) returned home for good. I assumed that during the time when he was away, he was living with someone else. Until then, he had never admitted that he didn't actually have anyone. The interesting thing is that when he finally confessed that I didn't feel sad nor did I feel that pain in my heart that I felt before. On the contrary, I felt such an unexplainable peace because I knew that My Beloved was in control of everything and I was so very grateful that He had kept me from knowing this before.

Other difficult moments were when my EH (earthly husband) asked me to appear in the public defender's office because he wanted to file for divorce. It was 2 times that he made this request both times my Beloved saved me.

Alana, what was the "turning point" of your restoration?

The turning point for sure was when I let go in my heart. I was living with my HH (Heavenly Husband) fully satisfied and told Him that I was willing to live with Him if that was His will because if I could choose, I'd choose Him. So very shortly after that my EH (earthly husband) came home. It was a Friday and he asked to spend the night with us and said he wanted to move his things back in. As this had already happened at other times, I did not have expectations on Saturday. Early that morning, the pastor's wife called me and asked if she could come over and talk to me at home. She came and said that my EH (earthly husband) had sought out her husband, our pastor, the prior week and she shared that my EH (earthly husband) opened up with our pastor. Her husband said that he didn't even look like the same person when he walked into his office. Before this, he was a totally cold person who didn't even answer the pastor's calls anymore, and for years they'd been very close friends. She said that my EH (earthly husband) cried and said that his life was terrible, so the pastor said that it was time for him to return home and to his family and never look back.

Tell us HOW it happened, Alana? Did your husband just walk in the front door? Alana, did you suspect or could you tell you were close to being restored?

Well, he just showed up on Friday. At first I said nothing. My EH (earthly husband) didn't tell me but I heard what happened during the conversation with my pastor's wife. She said my EH (earthly husband) confessed that he had been living with someone and although he was not entirely sure what he wanted, he said he wanted to be home with his family. I know it doesn't seem like a promising situation since he didn't come out and tell me himself, but the peace that my Beloved gave me during this conversation made me sure of our restoration. My Beloved has also shown me that I still have a long way to go, especially now that my EH (earthly husband) is at home. For he is not completely broken and has not yet returned to seek God the way he will need to. But I know that the One who started the work is the One who will complete it. My Beloved is mine and I am His, and He has done His will in my life. My family and marriage is His will and He is the One who I trust.

Would you recommend any of our resources in particular that helped you, Alana?

The books How God Can and Will Restore Your Marriage and A Wise Woman are extremely good. Both are filled with the wisdom of God. The course is most useful because it allows us to absorb each lesson more easily and to live what we learned. I also really enjoyed the second course, it has several lessons that were my favorites and I came back to them many, many times.

Would you be interested in helping encourage other women, Alana?

Yes. I have already filled out my application to be a minister in training to Become a Minister.

Either way, Alana, what kind of encouragement would you like to leave women with, in conclusion?

Search our Beloved. Don't worry about anything else. Your main role here on this journey is to meet your Heavenly Husband. Knowing Him is more important than trying to do the things you believe are right or even following the principles you're learning. Even if you slip with one or the other principle, if in your heart you seek your Beloved and have the desire to fulfill the principle the next time you will be successful and when you least imagine it happening, your marriage will be restored. Seek to be His Bride. Chase your Heavenly Husband more intensely than you chased your EH (earthly husband) or restoration and you will see your Beloved transforming everything before your eyes. It was like this for me and I pray and trust in the promises of my Beloved that it will also be like this with you to each who are reading my testimony today. Believe me, I know that He will.

Chapter 24

Jacelyn

"And unto the married I command
(yet not I, but the Lord):
let not the wife depart from her husband.
But if she depart, let her remain unmarried,
or be reconciled to her husband"
— 1 Corinthians 7:10-11

"My Once Rich and Successful EH Lost Everything"

Jacelyn, how did your Restoration Journey actually begin?

I have always believed I was a Christian. I was raised in the church and my parents were always God-fearing. I dated for about four years before and at 29 I married my EH (earthly husband). From the beginning there was a very big spiritual struggle because he came from a family who didn't really believe in God, unless they were low on money when they would pray for more.

Marriage was much more difficult than I could ever imagine, and have to say that my first year of marriage was terrible. However, I have always struggled to maintain my marriage and my family that hasn't changed. I knew he was a man of the world, but because he went to church with me and was fearful of God at the beginning, I thought it was okay that we marry.

After just a year, I had our first son and after another two years later, our daughter. With each new baby the difficulties, fights and trials increased, but I always believed that one day he would change or that God would change him and He was listening to my prayers. Of course at the time I never dreamed I was the one who needed changing.

Early on he was unfaithful, then he got so bold that he started to commit adultery inside our own home, he even harassed our children's nannies but I always forgave him when he said he was going to change.

Needless to say, he never changed. Each time I caught him and confronted him, it only made everything a hundred times worse.

Next, he left us and spent 2 months with OW (other woman), and then I heard she had been pregnant (which is why he left to live with her) and shortly after, he had a daughter. I suffered a lot, but what was worse is how much our son suffered. By this time he was 10 years old, so he already understood things.

One day after he was tired of the OW (other woman) and their new family, he came to me and asked if he could come home so I accepted (trusting him not trusting God that I learned we needed to do later), "Thus says the Lord, 'Cursed is the man who trusts in mankind and makes flesh his strength, and whose heart turns away from the Lord. For he will be like a bush in the desert and will not see when prosperity comes, but will live in stony wastes in the wilderness, a land of salt without inhabitant. Blessed is the man who trusts in the Lord and whose trust IS THE LORD. For he will be like a tree planted by the water, That extends its roots by a stream And will not fear WHEN the heat comes; but its leaves will be green, and it will not be anxious in a year of drought nor cease to yield fruit." Jeremiah 17:5-8

So we started again and at first, I thought he was going to change, however, more than two years later he had become much worse. I discovered he'd entered the social networks and fell into a world of unimaginable prostitution. I wrote more about this but remembered it is important to remain discreet not advertising what the enemy is doing "It is shameful even to talk about the things that ungodly people do in secret." Ephesians 5:12 NLT.

Well, as you teach here "For on account of a harlot one is reduced to a loaf of bread, and an adulteress hunts for the precious life. Can a man take fire to his bosom, and his clothes not be burned? The one who commits adultery with a woman is lacking sense; he who would destroy himself does it. Wounds and disgrace he will find, and his reproach will not be blotted out." Proverbs 6:24–33 my once rich and successful EH (earthly husband) lost everything, his job, and position, friends because he was so focused on a virtual world of sin. He never left his cell phone, night and day. One day I couldn't stand it and told him to leave the house. When he left he went to live in another city with his sister, then just after 2 weeks, he started dating OW (other woman) that he met through these social networks. I heard she was 10 years older than him and was a rich widow, so the doors the enemy opened for him were very wide.

I grieved a lot after this especially after being publicly humiliated and because he'd taken his other daughter (from the OW (other woman) born out of wedlock, which I had forgiven) and then began posting pictures of himself with the rich widow and his other daughter sharing everything with his family. Then at various times there were pictures of their many trips.

How did God change your situation, Jacelyn, as you sought Him wholeheartedly?

It all changed once the suffering became so severe that an aunt of mine gave me the book "How God Can and Will Restore Your Marriage", I read it immediately then reread it about 4 times, when GOD turned me upside down and inside out! Before this book, I just looked at his sin, then I started to see how I was foolish, quarrelsome, and everything else that a man didn't like in a woman (regardless of his sin), God spoke deeply to me through this book, from there I entered on the RMI website. I took all your courses, and everything you had to offer. I started my day with the devotionals, purchased all the books with the testimonies, reading the word of God daily and in 3 months read through the entire bible for the first time in my life. Each and everything offered was like medicine that I took daily to keep myself alive and in the presence of God. Over time, I realized that God had removed him from my life so that HE would be my first love for the first time. I never really knew the Lord, didn't realize God was my Father, but when all that changed, so did I!

What principles, from God's Word (or through our resources), Jacelyn, did the Lord teach you during this trial?

During this ordeal, He used you to teach me several principles, the most important and difficult for me were "winning without words" and "letting go." However, as you tell everyone, I sought God a lot and acknowledged He was restoring me, molding me. Most precious is that I found the love that I could never feel from anyone else. I finally felt what a Lover felt like, so much that I doubted if I wanted the restoration of my marriage because my HH (Heavenly Husband) was everything to me. The people around me were shocked to see just how much I was changing. The old contentious woman was no longer in me.

What were the most difficult times that God helped you through, Jacelyn?

The most difficult hours were when I saw his and OW's (other woman) pictures spread on all social networks, I didn't have social media anymore, after letting go of it but my family and friends watched and kept commenting or wanting to show me! Also when he disappeared, seeing our children and the suffering mainly with our son, was very difficult. He became very sick, almost went into a deep depression. To help, the OW (other woman) gave him a lot of money, material things, like cars, motorbikes, trips, pretending that his dad's life was perfect.

Then, after a year and a half living there with the other woman, my EH (earthly husband) asked me for a divorce because he said he needed this to allow him to secure a land deal with the OW (other woman). I didn't fight, I didn't hesitate, I simply agreed with my adversary, giving him everything he asked for and ask God how I could give more as the principle says we are to do. After I signed, I simply asked the Lord to get rid of the divorce, but that if it wasn't possible, if this was His plan, then to please just help me get through it enthusiastically as the book says.

Jacelyn, what was the "turning point" of your restoration?

Right after the divorce he already showed signs that things there were no longer going well, however, I said that he would only come back if it were by the hand of God and not by mine. I understood as a divorced woman, God gave us the option in 1 Corinthians 7:11 to either be reconciled or to live as His bride "she must remain unmarried, or else be reconciled to her husband...she is happier if she remains as she is."

Even though I didn't want restoration, I wanted above all for His will not mine. So I always spoke to him when he texted me and said that his life had turned into hell and that nothing in his life was working, that he wanted to get rid of OW (other woman) and that he couldn't stand living anymore, and that he was sorry. I just listened and said very little.

Tell us HOW it happened, Jacelyn? Did your husband just walk in the front door? Jacelyn, did you suspect or could you tell you were close to being restored?

Well, it's been close to three months since we married again, yes, the Lord showed me he would be coming back and to make the most of the time I had left alone with Him. So I did. And to make sure just to confirm that he wasn't just stopping here but would be off, I did wait before submitting my testimony.

I submitted praise reports each time things began to happen. He also left things behind because he had no money to bring them back home, then we heard she'd given all his things to charity posting it on social media. I knew that Erin and several testimonies that I read said that it would not be easy, that the enemy was going to provoke and that has been the case. Ever since he returned the fights started again, but this time I say nothing and just speak to my Lover when he goes off.

Would you recommend any of our resources in particular that helped you, Jacelyn?

How God Can and Will Restore Your Marriage, I have already gifted more than 12 women with this book and just ordered a case from your bookstore to give away. There are so many women who need and want this book after they saw what God did for me. I also love the book A Wise Woman and began a small group that meets in a nearby park so we can bring our children. I love the devotionals, too, and have continued the daily reading of the Word of God and hope to get through it again finishing at the end of the month. Everything you offer has helped and transformed me a lot.

Would you be interested in helping encourage other women, Jacelyn?

Yes

Either way, Jacelyn, what kind of encouragement would you like to leave women with, in conclusion?

Besides sharing what He's done for me and reading my testimony, I don't know what more I can say to help encourage other women. I suppose to say follow what all of us did is where to start and to notice how much having a HH (Heavenly Husband) is needed not just to complete the journey and be restored, but because you will need Him more after you're restored. The more you understand and experience Him as your Lover, the happier you will be no matter your circumstances

Chapter 25

Belina

"God is my salvation; I will have confidence and I will not fear.
The Lord, yes, the Lord is my strength and my song;
He is my salvation!"
—Isaiah 12:2

"Like All Feminists, I Complained Because He Didn't Help Me"

Belina, how did your Restoration Journey actually begin?

Almost a year into this journey, God surprised me with my miracle, today I can say my marriage has been fully restored. It all started when I thought everything was fine, I trusted my husband fully when he started to work with his parents in a small town, close to where we lived. It interfered with our life at home and I continually either harassed him too much about it or I teased him, because I wanted him to work here, in our city, sleeping at home every day with me. We had a daughter who was just turning 2 and he had so little contact with her, besides like all feminists, I complained because he didn't help me (even though he was supporting us I wanted him to do my job too). In addition, I complained, I had to keep coming and going to where he worked, it took our marriage a lot, I started going less where he was, he almost never came home, where he was working. What really got to me is when I got there, he wasn't at home but in bars and when he was at home he was on his cell phone and he didn't talk or look at me anymore when I spoke to him (of course I wasn't loving just ranting).

Even though I have been a Christian and gone to so many retreats for women, I did not know what God said about being a wife, and worse, I did not have a real relationship with God. One day God spoke to me in a dream, in the dream I experienced everything that actually happened. I woke up desperate, hysterically crying. I had closed my eyes to what was happening. I thought I could do and act any way I wanted and he would never betray me. After all, I thought I was an exemplary woman, but I was stupid. I was tearing down my house with my hands and didn't see it. I spoke with contempt, fought, accused, was bossy, thought I was the owner of our world, and was not submissive to my husband. God tried to warn me using people but I refused to see it! Until one day, my house fell. My husband was leaving me for an OW (other woman). I cried, screamed, fought, begged, and humiliated myself not to let this happen to us and to our daughter when she was so young. Nothing helped, he was gone. He moved into one of his father's houses, where he worked with OW (other woman). She had everything that was mine and was with my husband. It was at this time that I met RMI, looking for restored marriages on the net. I devoured the book How God Can and Will Restore Your Marriage in a week, I read and cried and reread and cried, each time the scales fell from my eyes and as I suffered from ignoring the truth, I was a contentious woman.

How did God change your situation, Belina, as you sought Him wholeheartedly?

Sisters, the secret is to shut up. It is to wait on God. I sought the Lord every day, all the time talking to Him, asking for wisdom, for discernment. The situation is too complicated for us to fight alone. God introduced me to a friend-sister, a true believer, who helped me a lot and helped me learn how to pray in my prayer closet, just me with Him. She knew what I was going through, she encouraged me, she agreed with me in prayer and often would fast with me.

"Therefore, confess your sins to one another, and pray for one another, that you may be healed. The plea of a righteous person can do a lot in his performance" (James 5:16). Stay away from all those who do not understand your situation, do not talk about your life or your husband, just don't talk to anyone but God! My colleagues never knew about my separation and it lasted almost 13 months. God is faithful sisters! He knew what was in my heart, that I didn't want anyone talking or commenting on my life and especially giving me stupid advice that got me here in the first place. During that time I dedicated myself entirely to the Lord, praying and praising without ceasing. That is why we fasted and begged this blessing from our God, and he answered us. "So we fasted and sought our God concerning this matter, and He listened to our pleading." Ezra 8:23

What principles, from God's Word (or through our resources), Belina, did the Lord teach you during this trial?

God spoke to me a lot, in all situations, before it happened He prepared me. I learned to be quieter, to think before I speak. I let go of anxiety and got busy with the things of the Lord. I encouraged other women to turn from feminism to becoming what God intended in order to be truly happy and had the opportunity to humble myself and confess my faults while sharing my testimony of tearing down my house. I begged them to turn to my Lord now before they lost their lives as I did and to speak of their problems only to Him and stop shaming their husbands. Sisters, we need to trust and believe in the Lord! He doesn't want to see us suffer, He loves us too much! He loves our husbands more than we do, so don't worry about anything. God will take care of everything! It is enough that you believe!

What were the most difficult times that God helped you through, Belina?

Seeing the photos that the OW (other woman) posted with my husband. Knowing that he was taking her to family gatherings. Having our daughter calling for her father all the time, and knowing that he chose to be away from us, killed me. My daughter got sick and became very ill and I was alone to take care of her—but through it all my Heavenly Husband supported me and drenched me with His love.

Belina, what was the "turning point" of your restoration?

I started to put into practice everything that was in the book and I read in each of your courses (I took them all, I became a student of the Word). I didn't care about anything or anyone else but the Lord. I didn't send messages no matter how tempted I was. He started to come twice a week to see our daughter, and I always made him comfortable with her and then left. As time went by he came and wanted to see me, wanted to be close to me, we talked, but I was always listening, agreeing, and soon he began to speak of his desire to return home. I stopped looking at the things that OW (other woman) published on Facebook (getting rid of my personal FB and opening one with my BNN so I could use it to minister to women and warn them). I didn't answer the OW (other woman) or any messages sent from her friend's phones, I just deleted them when I saw who they were coming from. I let go of my EH (earthly husband) completely in my heart! I truly delivered it to the Lord. Soon I no longer cared about the restoration of my marriage! I cared about my restoration with my Lover only! I just wanted my Heavenly Husband, in short, because my relationship with Him was pure and true, He was mine and I was His, that was more than enough for me. If this is not how you feel dear sister then this is what is in the way of your restoration and your happiness.

Tell us HOW it happened, Belina? Did your husband just walk in the front door? Belina, did you suspect or could you tell you were close to being restored?

One day, my husband came to visit our daughter and wanted to talk to me. He said he noticed how different I was and that I'd entirely changed. He said that I was calmer, more serene and that made him see that he still loved me and wanted to come home. Dear ones, I was so serene, I am entirely at peace, peaceful that I just said: "You need to be sure of what you want because I am very happy the way things are now." When I began my journey I imagined I would be jumping for joy, talking nonstop, but no! God was with me, He kept me quiet! My husband realized that I was happy and different! And I was! Because He was with me, He was all I needed! After we talked, it took another 21 days for him to come home. But I wasn't anxious and I didn't even call him. I put all my hope in the Lord and was grateful I had more time to be with Him. He knows the best for us! He knows the right time for everything! I believe this is when many fall down, fall back to their old ways, and begin to pine after their husbands, which breaks the heart of our Beloved and He knows He isn't able to return our husbands back home to their families.

Would you recommend any of our resources in particular that helped you, Belina?

Begin with the book How God Can and Will Restore Your Marriage, take each of the Courses, and get serious about your studies. Start your day with the Daily Devotionals. I point everyone to everything on your site! You are a gift from God and I treasure having been led here to RMI, I thank and praise for the life of Erin and for each woman who is part of this beautiful ministry!

Would you be interested in helping encourage other women, Belina?

Yes for sure. I pray daily and ask God to put women in my life who need help. I talk about my testimony, warn them and talk about how great God's love is for us!

Either way, Belina, what kind of encouragement would you like to leave women with, in conclusion?

My marriage has been restored by the Lord! That's all I can say! At first, it was not easy, the OW (other woman) sent me several messages, threatening me, lying that she was with him at all hours of the day and night (and blocking her didn't help) However, I did not answer (nor read) any message from her. I kept my eyes and hope on Him, praying, fasting, and soon falling in love with my Beloved HH (Heavenly Husband).

Dear ones, when our husband returns home the war is not over. When they come back is when the war really begins, so it's now that He's teaching you to focus on Him, to pray, and allow Him to intercede for us at all times! The enemy has lost and he does not like to lose, he will use everything he can to reach us, so we must always be on the side of HIM who can do all things! The Lord!!!!

Dear ones, I have been through what you are going through and I know how difficult it is! I read the testimonies and praised God for His love, and cried out that one day I would write my testimony! I dreamed of writing and shouting MY MARRIAGE HAS BEEN RESTORED BY THE LORD! Believe it!!! Trust!!!! Truly surrender everything to God!

Dear friend, He loves you! HE wants the best for you and your family! Many may say that their marriage is hopeless (I hear this a lot), but don't believe me, believe Him that YOUR MARRIAGE can be restored. YES! God can RESTORE your marriage!!!! Just trust! Shut up! Let go! Let go of everything that keeps you from the Lord! Say to the Lord, "You are my refuge and my strength, my God, in whom I trust". Psalm 91:2 "God is my salvation; I will have confidence and I will not fear. The Lord, yes, the Lord is my strength and my song; He is my salvation!" Isaiah 12:2 Say, "Even if I walked through the valley of the shadow of death, I would fear no harm, because You are with me, Your rod and Your staff comfort me." Psalm 23:4

Chapter 26

Arina

"I would have fainted, unless I had believed that I would see
the goodness of the Lord in the land of the living.
Wait on the Lord; be of good courage,
and He shall strengthen thine heart.
Wait, I say, on the Lord!"
—Psalms 27:13,14

"The Two of Us Were Still Sharing
the Same Bed"

Arina, how did your Restoration Journey actually begin?

We had been married for almost 19 years when I started to feel that things were not going well between us. My EH (earthly husband) was cold and distant. I, who was still a contentious and a VERY silly woman, started to confront him, always asking what was happening to him, trying to force him to talk, and this, of course, only made things worse between us. Then, in November, on my birthday, I was sure that there was something very wrong. The man who was always very affectionate and attentive, on that day of all days, was extremely cold and only celebrated my birthday by "obligation." From that day on (until I found your ministry), I started desperately looking for evidence of what was going on, and as God says, when you seek you will find!

Finding out that he was with OW (other woman) and as if that weren't enough, she was my "friend" at work, I went ballistic. I insanely confronted him, asking for an explanation, I called the OW (other woman) (how crazy). However, both denied it and there was no way to prove it. Even though they both denied it, I was sure it was true, so my world collapsed. From then on, things got worse and worse. My jealousy, regular confrontations and just being a bit insane, he got more and more distant and I got hurt every day and buried myself even more in my foolishness.

As I already knew God (from hearing about Him but not having a true personal relationship with Him or His Son) and truly believed that marriage was for life. I started to turn to Him, however, I neglected to give up my destructive behavior. And the more I tried to resolve it in my own strength, the more my marriage fell apart. At each of the December parties, including our wedding anniversary (which was this month), I felt empty and powerless. Everything he did left me feeling horrible: if he was cold I would fall apart, if he was attentive, I thought it was fake and was disgusted.

How did God change your situation, Arina, as you sought Him wholeheartedly?

It was in the month of January when I discovered some of his conversations with OW (other woman) about their relationship and they even talked about child custody; and even worse, I discovered this the night before his birthday, after all the celebrations were scheduled. I had the most challenging night of my life, my desire was to end all lies. I decided I would enjoy the event, then in front of all our friends and family I would "tell-all" and show everyone just "who he was"! But it was on that day that the Lord began to break me.

I spent the night battling with the Lord, as He began to show me who I really was! That I was responsible for everything that was happening. I started to see mySELF, the size of my EGO, that led to the quarrelsome, contentious, Pharisee, hypocritical woman and "owner of the world" person that I was. I understood that I had been deceiving people for a long time, demonstrating a "holiness" that was not true. In fact, I was managing to deceive myself. I also understood that the real reason why I was going through this situation was because the Lord had been trying to get my attention for a long time and I did not give any true importance to Him.

From that night on, the Lord began to shape my character, and I have since decided that I would only take a step IF I went with the Lord's permission. And my first attitude in total obedience to my Beloved Lord, was to keep all plans for my husband's birthday celebrations, because my HH (Heavenly Husband) told me that I should honor him, regardless of his behavior. (How difficult it was I can never describe.) Since then, I have been coming day after day, completely surrendering to my HH (Heavenly Husband) and I have found that nothing, absolutely nothing, is more important to me than Him. How I praise and thank You for not giving up on me, beloved of my soul. "How happy is the man you discipline, Lord, the one you teach your law to." Psalms 94:12 "Were it not for the Lord's help, I would already be dwelling in silence." Psalm 94:17

What principles, from God's Word (or through our resources), Arina, did the Lord teach you during this trial?

There were so many principles that I learned that I can't even list them, but some were critically fundamental in my Restoration Journey. Even before I threw myself into the arms of my HH (Heavenly Husband), I already understood that I shouldn't share any of this with anyone, except Him. However, the Word of God and the resources of RMI, strengthened me in this decision, and so, this was one of the principles that I manage to keep faithfully and still keep today. "Our help is in the Lord, who made the heavens and the earth." Psalms 124.8 Keeping silent (winning without words) and not seeking explanations from my EH (earthly husband) , is one of the most difficult principles to maintain, but the Lord has sustained me. "In the same way, women, each subject yourself to your husband, so that if he does not obey the word, he will be won without words." 1 Peter 3: 1 Another principle that has made a lot of difference in my Restoration Journey is not to be contentious, instead to try to be kind and gentle. "It is better to live in the desert than with a quarrelsome and embittered woman." Proverbs 21:19 "Pleasant words are like a honeycomb, are sweet to the soul and bring healing to the bones." Proverbs 16:24

What were the most difficult times that God helped you through, Arina?

Great were the struggles waged in this process of restoration, but the Lord has never forsaken me. Even when I wanted to give up, and throw it all away, my Beloved and beautiful HH (Heavenly Husband) took care of me, as I had never been taken care of. "It strengthens the tired and gives great strength to those who are weak." Isaiah 40:29 The turmoil of emotions I faced after discovering that my marriage was not as solid as everyone thought it was, was practically maddening. And I struggled against my mind that insisted on wanting to dissect and discuss every scene that I had become aware of, even though I hadn't seen anything. But at those times I poured myself into the loving arms of my HH (Heavenly Husband) and he always quieted my heart and made me know that everything was in HIS control and made me see the beautiful things He was planning for me.

Arina, what was the "turning point" of your restoration?

One day, after a very difficult week, with many struggles at work and countless completely unpleasant discoveries, I said a prayer to the Lord giving up everything. I said that I couldn't stand to fight for my marriage anymore, that I was basically giving up and that I was no longer interested in restoration. My focus and lessons would be only to get closer to Him. I said that everything was up to Him, and that all my prayers now would be just to get closer to Him.

That very same day, I discovered that my EH (earthly husband) had blocked the OW (other woman) on our social network page (we share the same page that I never logged into but was informed by another friend). I was so amazed that I had no words to thank my Beloved, as this was one of the requests I made most in my prayers early on. Only then did I realize that I was really understanding the principle of leaving my HH (Heavenly Husband) in control of everything and that He knew exactly the right time and every detail of my restoration journey.

In the days that followed, I also noticed that my EH (earthly husband) had deleted the OW (other woman) contact from his cell phone. I want to make it clear, that I had access to this information by chance, that I was not "snooping" (lol). In fact, I believe that my Beloved provided everything for me to know this information because He was saying softly to me: "Rest on Me, I know what you need and I am taking care of everything." Our HH (Heavenly Husband) is beautiful and I have no words to describe how much I am in love with Him.

Tell us HOW it happened, Arina? Did your husband just walk in the front door? Arina, did you suspect or could you tell you were close to being restored?

My EH (earthly husband) never left the house, our detachment happened with the two of us still sharing the same bed, which was extremely difficult. After I discovered the RMI and started to apply the principles contained in the available materials and in the Bible (which I can no longer distance myself from as His Word is everything to me), things started to change. I stopped being contentious, started living and taking pleasure in submitting to my EH (earthly husband) and, consequently, he got closer to me. We went back to talking about any topic and laughing together. But I still felt insecure, as I knew that contact with OW (other woman) had not ceased. However, days after I found out that he had blocked all contact with OW (other woman), we were returning from an exam, which he had to do but he insisted that I accompany him, when he started talking to me about OW (other woman).

Among many things that he declared to me that he could no longer bear to have contact with her, that they had had a final discussion (sounded like a violent fight), and that he took the opportunity to exclude and block her from every means possible and from that moment on, he was asking God to strengthen him to that he would not go back and that the Lord would restore everything that had been lost!! Can you imagine how stunned I was to hear those words?

My EH (earthly husband) went on to say that because he wanted to walk according to the Lord's purposes for our marriage and especially for His life, he wanted to become the man of God he should be and (basically) become my spiritual leader (just not in those exact words). We had an amazing conversation with me saying little to nothing, just nodding and smiling.

I praise my Beloved because He helped me manage and control my emotions while keeping silent. "Despite this, I have this certainty: I will live until I see the Lord's goodness on earth. Wait on the Lord. Be strong! Courage! Wait on the Lord." Psalm 27:13,14

Would you recommend any of our resources in particular that helped you, Arina?

Yes, absolutely! I recommend that you read the books "How God Can and Will Restore Your Marriage" and then be sure to read the "Wise Woman" if you really believe your marriage will be restored because it gets you ready for this to happen. I also recommend each of the Abundant Life Courses, reading the Devotionals and daily encourager each morning before the lessons. But I mainly recommend the daily reading of the Bible, where you will be sure of everything that the materials available at RMI contain. "Rather, he takes pleasure in the law of the Lord, and in His law he meditates day and night." Psalm 1:2

Would you be interested in helping encourage other women, Arina?

Yes, certainly.

Either way, Arina, what kind of encouragement would you like to leave women with, in conclusion?

First of all, understand that this journey of restoration is not about the restoration of your marriage solely and exclusively. In fact, this was the way the Lord knew would draw you to Him and get your attention. So, if you haven't already, immediately start putting God where He should always be, at the center, and above all, in control of your life. I can guarantee that you will experience the greatest experience of your entire life. And never give up! Divorce should not be an option. But if it happens (or happened), stay strong, because our God is a specialist in turning a curse into a blessing. "And we know that all things work together for the good of those who love God, of those who are called according to his purpose." Romans 8:28

Chapter 27

Calista

"A continual dripping on a very rainy day
and a contentious woman are alike."
—Proverbs 27:15

"At the Door, My Husband, Tears Running Down His Face"

Calista, how did your Restoration Journey actually begin?

I think things started deteriorating even before we got married. I always had a very strong "temperament" (nice word for nothing more than horribly contentious) and from the beginning, when we were dating, I argued with my husband about things that I didn't think were right and even if they weren't really anything worth arguing about. The bible teaches us to act entirely differently, which I didn't do and so I took all of that into our marriage.

How did God change your situation, Calista, as you sought Him wholeheartedly?

When my husband left home, I was in shock. To me, although I was contentious and we fought over everything, most recently financial issues, we were always friends. We had loved each other since childhood, so it was very difficult to grasp. Since I was a child I have been a Christian and so in the midst of everything, God was appealing to me showing me everything I did wrong. So I repented to the Lord, then I repented and asked my husband for forgiveness. Every day I sought God more, to understand what He wanted me to do, to make Him not only my Savior, but also my Lord. So after about a month when my husband had left home, I found the book How God can and will restore your marriage and the book only confirmed everything that God was already ministering to my heart but now He provided me with a roadmap to get through my Restoration Journey.

What principles, from God's Word (or through our resources), Calista, did the Lord teach you during this trial?

Several!! First of all it was to love my God over all things, that was fundamental in my life. He needed to be and now is my everything: my best friend, my protector, my Husband, the reason for my life, all I need is Him and all I want is Him. Becoming His bride changed my life and for this, I will be forever grateful to RMI. Now I can no longer live a second without His presence, without His love pouring over me.

The principle of goodness, especially goodness coming from my mouth, which is a reflection of my heart. Having a gentle and quiet spirit was what made my husband notice something different about me. Praise God the contentious woman was gone and he couldn't believe it. Sometimes he even said "It is not possible for someone to be like this, you are kidding me, this is not serious. This kindness is fake." But what my EH (earthly husband) saw was Him and His love in me and that was real.

Letting go and winning without words, these are also fundamental. I did not question my husband as to where he was, with whom he was with, whether he would return, I gave everything into the hands of God and rested in Him.

What were the most difficult times that God helped you through, Calista?

When he told me about OW (other woman) and the possibility that she was pregnant. It left me devastated, and in the moments when I thought things would flow and he said he could not leave OW (other woman) and he felt guilty and accused by the enemy. In those moments I poured myself out to the Lord, I always cried only to Him, alone. Through it all, I never doubted what He had said to my heart that He would do, the tears were my heart breaking. I was so thankful that every time I faced some more news that was not in my favor, the Lord, my Husband, gave me peace in my heart that exceeded all my understanding. There is no way to explain it. He's wonderful and I love Him so much.

Calista, what was the "turning point" of your restoration?

The turning point was when I decided to let go of restoration entirely, my new purpose was a life alone with the Lord. My prayers also changed. At dawn to cry out for my husband's salvation, for 7 days (perfection number for completion), I got up at dawn to cry out for my husband's salvation, so that He would have an encounter with God. At the end of the 7th day I heard someone at the door and when I went to open it, to my surprise, it was my husband, tears running down his face. How can I express to you what I felt, how I felt the power of God and how He heard my prayers and how I was able to rejoice in my husband's salvation. Never even believing in God, due to my complete transformation and my prayers for Him, God performed a miracle. I love my HH (Heavenly Husband) more than anything in my life and I am nothing and nothing at all without Him, I love You, Lord, I love You! My husband moved back home that day after 22 months away from home.

Tell us HOW it happened, Calista? Did your husband just walk in the front door? Calista, did you suspect or could you tell you were close to being restored?

I did not suspect that he would return exactly the day I finished purposely praying for his salvation, but I had expectations that God would do something amazing. I deeply believed that my purpose would be served by God, as a single woman after reading this in the Message Bible (after becoming a lover of all versions that I devoured all day long).

"Sometimes I wish everyone were single like me—a simpler life in many ways! But celibacy is not for everyone any more than marriage is. God gives the gift of the single life to some, the gift of the married life to others.

"I do, though, tell the unmarried and widows that singleness might well be the best thing for them, as it has been for me. But if they can't manage their desires and emotions, they should by all means go ahead and get married. The difficulties of marriage are preferable by far to an emotionally tortured life as a single.

"And if you are married, stay married. This is the Master's command, not mine. If a wife should leave her husband, she has two choices, she must either remain single or else come back and make things right with him.

"For the rest of you who are in mixed marriages—Christian married to non-Christian—we have no explicit command from the Master. So this is what you must do...If you are a woman with a husband who is not a believer but he wants to live with you, hold on to him. The unbelieving husband shares to an extent in the holiness of his wife... Otherwise, your children would be left out; as it is, they also are included in the spiritual purposes of God.

On the other hand, if the unbelieving spouse walks out, you've got to let him or her go. You should not hold on desperately. God has called us to make the best of it, as peacefully as we can. You never know, wife: The way you handle this might bring your husband not only back to you but to God." 1 Corinthians 7:7-16

I was sure that He would be faithful and trusted His will for my life and for my husband's life. That day, my husband came home with all his things, Glory be to God, all honor and all glory! His heart has never strayed from me or the Lord whom he serves.

Would you recommend any of our resources in particular that helped you, Calista?

Yes, the book How God Can and Will Restore Your Marriage was the best thing that God could have given to me at that time, that book changed my way of seeing and allowed me to repent of my sins and open my heart for the Lord to me. From there, to shape according to His will, I took all but one of your courses, which I am currently doing now. My husband also is studying a Wise Man.

Would you be interested in helping encourage other women, Calista?

Yes, I believe that is why God allowed me (and every woman He leads here) to go through all of this, so that I could help other women and people (I've given the RYM for men who are in the same situation and point them to Hope At Last site. What I want most is to bless other lives so that there is restoration in their lives, not just marriages, so the Lord is glorified

Either way, Calista, what kind of encouragement would you like to leave women with, in conclusion?

Don't give up, no matter what your husband says, what people say, whatever anyone says or you see or you hear. No matter what, focus on God, He wants your marriage restored more than you do. If you pour your heart out at the Lord's feet and then as you rise up and later sit on His lap as His Lover, pay attention to do everything according to His will. Let go of your plan. Rest in Him and then you will see the miracle happen. Our God is a God of miracles, and when your marriage is restored, give Him all the honor, all the praise and all Glory. Focus on helping others. Do not give up!!!

Chapter 28

Evelyn

"You oh God have removed my acquaintances far from me;
You have made me an object of loathing to them;
I am shut up and cannot go out."
—Psalm 88:18

"An Object of Loathing"

Evelyn, how did your Restoration Journey actually begin?

It started unexpectedly. My EH and I are pastors and married 12 years next month. We always talked, we had a lot of fun, and we were examples for other couples, especially young people. At the end of last year, he started to distance himself. I work on Saturdays, and every Saturday when I arrived back home, he was there at home with our baby as they went to the mall every Saturday and he didn't want me to go with him. He kept getting more and more distant, he didn't pay attention to me as before and then he would start a fight saying that we were having a boring relationship. Believe it or not, I thought everything was "normal" what every couple went through and despite the signs, I thought all was fine. Then suddenly in February, my world collapsed. One day he began to shout at me and said he was no longer my husband, out of nowhere he said that I could no longer call him a husband because he was no longer my husband. I did not know what to do, I suffered tremendously because I thought I had the perfect marriage. And after that he started treating me like a stranger, actually worse, like a person that he hated, just ignored, or shouted at, horribly mistreated. But it was clear that this was not my EH, that I was dealing with something worse. After reading the book, I understood when my EH said he was no longer my husband, because all along I had an HH. A Husband I had ignored and mistreated.

How did God change your situation, Evelyn, as you sought Him wholeheartedly?

I discovered the book How God can restore your marriage and everything in my life changed. I started to see the fool that I was and how selfish I was, I was the head of the house, not my EH. Like all women I gloried in being in charge, being a strong woman when I was nothing but a fool. I recognized my mistakes and thought that everything would change, but things got worse and worse, and there was a huge chasm, a void between us. The only person I had was my HH, I just talked, cried, prayed, with HIM and our relationship grew to what it needed to be.

What principles, from God's Word (or through our resources), Evelyn, did the Lord teach you during this trial?

The principle of the Word of God that the woman must know to build their lives on. How could I have grown up in the church and gone through seminary, taught women and not have known anything that Erin taught is in her books? The beauty and freedom to be submissive to your husband "as unto the Lord" (meaning we can show our HH our love by doing what He asks and trusting Him). Also, that the husband is the head of the wife. And the book's principle of letting go, goodness, that was very difficult to grasp, but it worked, even though I was not seeing it happening, my Beloved was working. And keeping silent at all times was and still has been very difficult, but it really was the most precious principle, which avoids many pains. These principles aren't just for marriage either. The way He helped me practice them in every area of my life enriched my life beyond what I ever imagined.

What were the most difficult times that God helped you through, Evelyn?

It was to see my EH, who always had hurried home to see his family, always arriving very late. He left work at 6 in the morning and would arrive back home sometimes 22 or 23 hours later. In the beginning I asked if there was a meeting, he said no, he came late because he wanted to. He couldn't stand the sight of me. Thankfully I learned to remain silent soon after and saved myself a lot of pain. I became used to a lot of his rudeness, and the many times when he didn't look at me anymore, I was invisible. In this, the principle of letting go helped me a lot, because when I didn't ask, I wasn't mistreated and I didn't suffer.

Also understanding this very important principle "You have removed lover and friend far from me; My acquaintances are in darkness." and "You oh God have removed my acquaintances far from me; You have made me an object of loathing to them; I am shut up and cannot go out." Psalm 88:18-8.

Evelyn, what was the "turning point" of your restoration?

I was very afraid to write this testimony because in my heart my marriage was not yet restored. But today I took courage and wrote because, after 8 months of crisis, my EH never left home. Our pastor confided that he broke down crying and confessed that he had left a mattress in an empty apartment that we are trying to sell, and that he would leave home and live there. If I had not followed the principles I would have kicked him out of our house. Soon after he came to me and confessed the same thing but after he'd thrown away the mattress.

Tell us HOW it happened, Evelyn? Did your husband just walk in the front door? Evelyn, did you suspect or could you tell you were close to being restored?

My husband never left physically (only due to God's grace) because I'd been given the book and devoured the truth before I'd made the fatal mistakes of so many women I know and read about. There was no other woman, again only due to the grace of God. Today, he arrives home on time most days, except when he has an important meeting, we talk, he looks at me and we go to church together. Throughout he's remained to be a good father devoted to our son and I'm thankful has not missed anything due to tearing my house down. We are not yet in love but we are loving and caring towards one another. I let him lead in this and watch his cues. I would not have survived if I didn't have the love of my HH because he is all I need and my EH's love and attention is just an added blessing from my Heavenly Father.

Would you recommend any of our resources in particular that helped you, Evelyn?

I recommend all Erin's materials, especially the book How God Can and Will Restore Your Marriage. I share this book whenever I can with anyone who will listen. There is a friend from work who was fired last week who hugged me and said that maybe she only worked at that shop (where I'd go get coffee) so that on the day she needed it, I handed her the book and told her not to do anything stupid. Today her marriage is completely restored, and she purchased A Wise Woman to learn how to take care of her family. Hallelujah!

Would you be interested in helping encourage other women, Evelyn?

I'm already helping but I always want to help more. It's our duty to spread the truth and save the marriages that are collapsing. We need to be armed with books to give, the site to send them to and the love He bathes us in to be aware of who needs our help.

Either way, Evelyn, what kind of encouragement would you like to leave women with, in conclusion?

Girls, don't give up! As difficult as it may seem, the loneliness and the feelings of contempt that invade your heart, know that your heart is deceitful. Because your Beloved is working on your behalf, He wants you to trust Him, love Him and make Him your Lover and if you don't do that, if you don't trust, there is no reason for Him to work on your behalf. He loves you more than you could imagine and takes care of every detail of your life. Count this journey in the desert as a blessing and enjoy what He's called you to do.

Chapter 29

Davina

"Humble yourselves, therefore, under God's mighty hand,
that he may lift you up in due time."
—1 Peter 5:6

"After His Third Proposal and We Remarried"

Davina, how did your Restoration Journey actually begin?

It all started because I was a difficult woman to be around and everyone who knew me would laugh because of the woman who prided herself as having no control and refused to be in submission to anyone or anything. After I married, I was obsessed and I only thought about my husband 24 hours a day, what he was doing and thinking. I also fought a lot. But my EH was always good to me, until he got tired of me and the things I did, and I sensed he'd emotionally left me after he lost interest. Next he said he didn't love me anymore and wanted to see me as far away from him as he could get. When I looked into his eyes, he looked through me as if I was nothing. All the feelings that I expressed to him were ignored and not reciprocated. Everything got worse, and when I tried to hold on to him and not the Lord, because I was needy and confused and couldn't make any sense of the lonely nights and dreary weekends alone, I became like a mad crazed woman. Like a wild wounded animal. While everything was falling apart I sensed there was joy on the other side, but I didn't know that this was God's way of drawing me to Him and rescuing me from all that unbearable pain and the woman who I was and who everyone despised, myself included.

How did God change your situation, Davina, as you sought Him wholeheartedly?

When I didn't know what to do anymore, tired of trying, of crying, of regret, I told my HH "let YOUR will be done" because I don't want to keep suffering like this. I didn't want to miss my ex-husband, because we got divorced when he had enough of me.

What principles, from God's Word (or through our resources), Davina, did the Lord teach you during this trial?

Read the Bible day and night, night and day and declare the Word as your truth. Be sure to pray and fast. I also read how God can and will restore your marriage several times and started the courses which are very good to keep you moving forward and changing.

What were the most difficult times that God helped you through, Davina?

At that time everything was difficult for me, it was unbearable pain when I felt the pain of rejection, the neediness. I thought I would never have a family like I'd dreamed of because I was divorced and I found out about the OW. When I begged him not to leave me alone, when he asked me not to drink anymore and so many situations that were crashing down in my life that I cried due to so much pain, mainly the pain in my soul.

Davina, what was the "turning point" of your restoration?

That's when I left everything in God's hands and didn't want to think about my ex-husband anymore. I fully truly let go.

Tell us HOW it happened, Davina? Did your husband just walk in the front door? Davina, did you suspect or could you tell you were close to being restored?

We were married for 12 years and from the start, it was very difficult. I was a foolish person but my husband was always affectionate and I, in my ignorance, did everything wrong and ended up making him walk away from me. After I confessed my mistakes to him, everything got worse, he started to go out and come back at dawn and leave me until one day he asked me for a divorce. Oh I cried and cried to God and I searched the internet for a way to alleviate my pain, and with God's mercy, I found RMI and followed the principles of the Bible found in the book God can and will restore your marriage.

I was devastated fighting to get my marriage back and the more I wanted it the more I despised myself and ended up exhausted. I cried bitter tears, but my HH tried His best to get me to understand that God would do it. The book title says that but I just didn't get it. All too soon I fell into deep despair of being alone and thought of ending it all. The divorce was about to happen, then in one day it really happened, we actually got divorced, and that's when my HH opened my eyes and showed me how much I idolized not Him, but my EH. I thought about him all the time and left my true Love, setting Him aside. I understood that He wanted me, but I wanted my EH. So He removed lover and friend, and made me a loathing.

By this time I'd made my way through the first three courses but resisted the course I needed. I didn't want an abundant life without my husband. On the day I reached the end and was tempted to start course 1 again, I asked my HH to fill me with more of Him and help me release my grip on my ex, to fill me with forgiveness and not hold back kind words. From the moment we got married, even before that, my life consisted of fights, disputes, and out of control behaviour.

As I got closer to my beloved HH and the fear was draining out of my heart, because I felt my beautiful HH flow in me, over me and through me. I was still in my house, but he had already left and got involved, living with the OW, for which I was foolish to find out if it was true because I started a huge fight when I had found out and hurt myself and my journey even more, and knowing who she was, who my HH tried to shield me from, also hurt me a lot. So I went to live with my father, but it didn't work out as I'd hoped so soon I went to live with my mother, and it was with my mother that I spent close to four years healing and changing. I no longer worked or went out at all. I remained home, shut up with the Lord.

When I didn't have any more strength to pray for my marriage, I asked the Lord to have His will in my life, when out of nowhere my ex-husband showed up and started to come to my mother's house to visit us both. Soon after we started dating again and he asked me to marry him. I accepted after his third proposal and we remarried. All honor and glory to our Beloved HH.

Just a month later we discovered we were expecting our first child after the restoration and I knew it was time for me to write my testimony.

May I tell you my beloved friend that as Erin said, after the restoration it would not be easy, and it is true. Many old habits tried to dominate my life, the stresses of everyday life, the tiredness, and even small discouragements make me close to slipping into my old ways. Once my beloved slips to the background, rather than remaining first, I stumble. I have fallen several times but by the grace of my HH He is there and will always lift me up and finish what He started. He began giving me a new and abundant life. My God is who will fulfill His promises in my life because I do not want to be even an inch away from my beloved.

I am very grateful for His love, power and faithfulness in my life, thank You my HH for everything and know that each day I continue to hope that I may serve You in a much more meaningful way. This is another desire of my heart, to have my EH as passionate about Him as I am. He is not yet the spiritual leader of our home, but I believe he will soon be. I want my family founded on the Rock and I am content to wait. He has already fulfilled many of my hopes and desires so why not this one? Thank you very much, I love you my HH.

Would you recommend any of our resources in particular that helped you, Davina?

Yes, the Bible and the book How God Can and Will Restore Your Marriage is what helped me so much to keep my eyes on Him and keep my mouth shut. Also the book a wise woman and the courses. Everything on your site I know that everything was given to Erin to give to us to help us and edify us and transform us. Take the courses and read the books, this I pray in the name of the Lord.

Would you be interested in helping encourage other women, Davina?

Yes, for sure.

Either way, Davina, what kind of encouragement would you like to leave women with, in conclusion?

Do not give up, even if everything says it's hopeless, no matter how long it takes. Just think of how many years it took you to get to this state, this mess, so give Him time to heal and transform you and don't try to restore it yourself or be resistant to what is offered here as it will only prolong your healing and restoration. God says yes, and amen to restoration because what God has united man cannot truly separate. God is faithful and remains faithful, He fulfills everything He promises. When I was losing strength and hope, He lifted me up and helped me to continue trusting and so too God will do for you my beloved friend. Just believe, trust and surrender everything to our HH.

Chapter 30

Kaylie

"God can do anything, you know—
far more than you could ever imagine or guess
or request in your wildest dreams!"
—Ephesians 3:20

"Each Blessing Took the Hate-Wall Down Brick by Brick"

Kaylie, how did your Restoration Journey actually begin?

My husband and I met on Valentine's Day by a friend who intuitively introduced us and practically grabbed us both saying that we were meant for each other. He is European and was from Angola. I come from a Catholic Christian home, and he comes from a family where they know almost nothing about God whatsoever, and each said they had no intention of knowing anything.

I had already been married and I had a 2 year old son, while he was younger and without children. Our courtship started out wonderfully, it seemed like a romance novel, it was so romantic. Our first crisis started when in 2015 he decided to take me to Europe to meet his family, a family that was against the relationship for several reasons: race being the biggest factor. Also, the fact of my being married previously, me being older and already having a child. Anyway, the trip was a nightmare. Had I known what the Bible said about marriage, divorce, remarriage or honoring parents, I would have sought to restore my first marriage rather than look for a man who I would cause to commit adultery.

When we got back to Angola he became obsessively jealous, he searched my social networks and said that men only wrote to me because I was this and that, he offended me in every way. I discovered in him a man quite manipulated by his mother, she manipulated him so perfectly that even he himself did not notice. Little by little, with so much jealousy and mistrust, he became a cold and distant man, and I started to neglect myself (we were already living together even without marrying something else I was ignorant about). To combat his behaviour I became an increasingly arrogant, quarrelsome woman, fitting the mold of the contentious woman and other times I'd turn cold.

Then to save his sanity, he decided to move out, but at the time I was 5 months pregnant with our daughter. Then ended with what I refer to as my "first restoration" as I was restored and in December he returned to live together so he was there when our daughter was born.. But I was a foolish woman. Soon after the restoration, I turned back and started back to my own ways.

Nevertheless, we decided to marry for the sake of our daughter. Then shortly after my mother-in-law's visit, my marriage collapsed. I blamed her for the destruction, while ignorant that I had pulled it down with my own hands, a home, life and marriage that was built entirely on sinking sand.

I started to argue with my husband in front of his mother, I became furious, and people noticed I almost never smile anymore. I was always sad and sulky, pouting and then finally my husband had enough. He threw me out of the house with my son. Then he took out a restraining order and I was no longer able to even see my baby daughter. This is what I needed to turn my life around and God knew it.

How did God change your situation, Kaylie, as you sought Him wholeheartedly?

In my pain and fear, I poured out my heart to my Beloved, and God used each humiliating wound to humble me. It was with great pain and failure that I began to gradually feel the Lord embracing and calming me. I had already read the book How God Can and Will Restore Your Marriage a few times, but I read it again and burst into tears, because I realized that almost nothing I had read ever changed me during my first restoration, and I realized that I entirely ignored God's warnings about second marriages, which led me to this impossible marriage I was now trying to restore. Was it even His plan? Just the fact I wanted His plan, His will for my life was a huge milestone, a real awakening.

My Love knew I needed to go through this valley of tears, to show me how silly I was, how quarrelsome, contentious and unyielding I still am. The Lord began to wash me with His love, washing all the emotional and hurt wounds that I brought with me from the past and made me see the entire episodes in which I believed that my mother-in-law harmed me, to see how she, as a mother, wanted to protect her son just as much as I wanted to and should have protected my son (by not marrying or becoming involved with another man that was not his father).

This desert served to force me to be alone with my Beloved, to make me go back to where I have always been, in His arms. Today the Lord is my everything, I have realized what it is like to be intimate with a Heavenly Husband. Dear ones, He is so much closer than we imagine just wanting you to feel His embrace.

What principles, from God's Word (or through our resources), Kaylie, did the Lord teach you during this trial?

Winning without words, not defending myself but letting my HH (Heavenly Husband) do that for me. During this period, my husband was brutal, calling me out, offending and provoking me in every way, especially when I stopped my attacks. This one principle, winning without words, but giving a blessing instead, helped me to realize that the fight was never against my husband (or my mother-in-law) but against the real enemy. So when my husband acted like that, I asked my Beloved how I might bless him and each time it softened his heart, taking the hate-wall down brick by brick.

What were the most difficult times that God helped you through, Kaylie?

The moment I left the house and tried to move into another apartment, my EH (earthly husband) told me he wouldn't give me a penny to help pay the rent or anything else. He actually went out of his way to take things away from me. Yet, the Lord helped me to remain calm and serene, confident, and just pray "Your will be done, Lord. He led me to stay at my parents' house for a month because I had nowhere to stay. But this was entirely His perfect plan as I was able to learn how to honor my parents and repent of the kind of daughter that I had been. I remember reading how living with parents, especially when there are children, is important to rebuild a more solid foundation, so I am thankful this was part of my restoration journey.

The other difficult time was when my husband removed me from Facebook, and then my mother and my friend came to tell me that he started to post several photos. Thankfully, I'd just finished the lesson on fasting facebook so I knew it was my Beloved protecting me. So I didn't have to see that my husband was clearly having an affair with a coworker, something that hurt me a lot at the time when I heard about it. But again God used it for my good to drive me into the arms of my Beloved HH (Heavenly Husband) which is where I needed to be.

Kaylie, what was the "turning point" of your restoration?

The turning point was when I realized that I would not be able to let go and tell God that I accepted that He may not want this marriage restored since it was a second marriage. I didn't know what that would mean for my children since they had two different fathers, but I knew I needed to let go and trust Him.

So I began praying only for His will. I prayed for days also saying, "Lord if this is not your will, take him out of my mind entirely and turn my heart away from him as well. Turn my heart towards You alone so I no longer have any feelings that make me want or miss him. I would repeat this so many times during the day and night. Then, one night I felt that from that moment on I had really let go. That night for the first time I stopped wanting restoration, and I truly desired the Lord to be my Husband and no one else. I truly wanted God's will for my life, whatever it was. As crazy as it may seem when I woke up the next day I had 2 missed calls from my husband and they were kind and loving. Then I got a text message a few hours later when I didn't call him back or contact him, saying that he was coming to visit us, after several months without any contact.

I knew it was God who was restoring because I really didn't want it, but I knew I needed to trust whatever He was about to do. I have to say that letting go is really powerful. As I write this, I just have to smile at how faithful He is. Thank you, my Beloved!

Tell us HOW it happened, Kaylie? Did your husband just walk in the front door? Kaylie, did you suspect or could you tell you were close to being restored?

My husband asked me to move back home two days after his first visit. Also, in order to not have any outside influence, we agreed that for now, it would be better to keep our situation to ourselves, so after the five months of being back together, neither of our families know about it. The fact we don't live in the same country as either of our families makes this possible. Both children are extremely happy and so far we haven't faced any real difficulties customary to restored marriages. Hopefully things will continue to be just a happy coexistence as we build our home and family on the Rock, even though my husband is not yet a believer. He has commented often at the change in me and each time I say it was God who did it, so I trust He will complete what He started and someday soon I will be submitting a praise report and a salvation story for you to share.

Would you recommend any of our resources in particular that helped you, Kaylie?

Glory to God, absolutely. First, the book How God Can and Will Restore Your Marriage, which is a gift from God above!! That book does not restore marriages, it restores us!!! The restoration of marriage is one of the "additions" that our Beloved gives us. I highly recommend reading this multiple times. "But seek first His kingdom and His righteousness, and all these things will be added to you." Matthew 6:33

Would you be interested in helping encourage other women, Kaylie?

Of course, I really want to grow in faith. And sharing my weaknesses is one of the best ways to grow! "And He has said to me, 'My grace is sufficient for you, for power is perfected in weakness." Most gladly, therefore, I will rather boast about my weaknesses, so that the power of Christ may dwell in me. Therefore I am well content with weaknesses, with insults, with distresses, with persecutions, with difficulties, for Christ's sake; for when I am weak, then I am strong.'" 2 Corinthians 12:9-11

Either way, Kaylie, what kind of encouragement would you like to leave women with, in conclusion?

Let EVERYTHING go in your life. Our Beloved is the One who knows how to take better care of us than we could ever imagine! "God can do anything, you know—far more than you could ever imagine or guess or request in your wildest dreams!" Ephesians 3:20

Chapter 31

Naomi

"Happy is the man who endures temptation.
Because, after suffering the trial,
he will receive the crown of life that God
has promised to those who love him"
—James1:12

"He Brought the OW on Vacation and I Hugged Her"

Naomi, how did your Restoration Journey actually begin?

My desert started about eight years ago while I was getting ready for my college exams. I found out through a cousin that my EH (earthly husband) was cheating on me. His whole family already knew. He took advantage of the fact that I was not going with him to his mother's house and told everyone that he was separated from me. Nobody understood and did not believe it. We have three children and have been married for 18 years. I say that we are married because despite all this he never left home even though he was with OW (other woman). He spent the week at home and on the weekends he went to her house. My EH (earthly husband) said he was going to travel for work, so he went on Saturday and returned on Monday. I didn't suspect anything. As I was Catholic (before becoming His bride), the day before I went to sleep, I was praying the rosary as usual, but when I finished praying, a message arrived on my cell phone. I used to turn it off every night but something didn't let me turn it off that day. I went to check the message and it was from my EH's niece. She said that she liked me a lot and that she was angry about what my EH (earthly husband) was doing to me. I didn't understand and asked what she meant. That was when she told me that he was going there every weekend and that the OW (other woman).was already being introduced as a wife to everyone.

My world collapsed and I slipped to the floor! We had just left a rental because we had built our house, so I never imagined that this would be happening in the midst of our new life. My reaction was like everyone here has said, I cursed, defamed him in front of the whole family, I did everything the other way around, cheating on him and all it did was make the situation get worse, much much worse because now my own guilt and shame was added on top of everything.

My EH (earthly husband) started to hate me. We argued incessantly; he said he didn't love me anymore, so my son tried to talk to him but he said there was no way. Yet God was so faithful that he didn't let him leave the house, nevertheless, my ordeal increased every day because I had to live with that situation. He spoke to OW (other woman) on the phone with such affection right in front of us that it made me feel horrible. He paraded with her everywhere and everyone in the family could not believe it because it was so unlike him.

So, without knowing anything about why this was all happening, why God allowed it to happen, I acted in the flesh, so as I said, the situation got so much worse. I lost nine kilos or 21 pounds in just a few weeks. I lost the will to live as if everything had no meaning in my life.

As I asked God why, that's when I remembered that just before all this happened, I had asked God to transform my EH (earthly husband), as he loved to spend weekends in bars and did not have time for the family, that's when God asked if I was prepared, I said yes. I was raised with great difficulty by a single mother, without a father, so I didn't want my children to go through this. I believed but it was not with FAITH. I started slandering my EH (earthly husband) by acting like a fool and that was driving him further away from our family. My husband was blinded in his sin, he didn't care about his children, he left them even more in need, it wasn't him.

I foolishly decided to call OW (other woman) not to attack her but just to talk. I feel ashamed when I remember what I did because all it did was to give her every weapon she needed to finish me off. His whole family was on my side, which was comforting, yet the OW (other woman) kept my EH (earthly husband) away from every member of his family, even his mother. It really wasn't my EH (earthly husband) in that body, he would never do that. Nothing made sense, how this could be God's plan and answer to my prayer until I stumbled on this while reading through the Bible with my ePartner, we both saw it. "A senseless man has no knowledge, Nor does a stupid man understand this: That when the wicked sprouted up like grass And all who did iniquity flourished, It was only that they might be destroyed forevermore." Psalm 92:6-7

How did God change your situation, Naomi, as you sought Him wholeheartedly?

I joined several groups through WhatsApp prayers but I couldn't find answers, but thank God I never stopped looking for you. About a year into my journey, I decided to give up on my marriage. That day I cried out to the Lord that I couldn't stand this situation anymore, my family had lost everything, I cried so much that day and asked the Lord to set me free.

So, in the WhatsApp group, there was a woman asking for prayer because she was going to make a decision about her marriage, that's when another woman asked her not to do this without first going to the website: www.HopeAtLast.com and my whole body shivered. I knew, just knew, that God heard my cries. Immediately when I started reading the book "How God can and will restore your marriage", I cried with joy. There was so much I didn't understand about marriage nor how to be a wife and certainly how to handle any crisis God's way. I had so much to learn!

What principles, from God's Word (or through our resources), Naomi, did the Lord teach you during this trial?

How much wealth of wisdom there was on your site. After I finished reading the eBook I ordered, I started taking your free courses and each day I got stronger spiritually and emotionally. There was a bible in the house but I never imagined that every solution to my situation would be there. "Happy is the man who endures temptation. Because, after suffering the trial, he will receive the crown of life that God has promised to those who love him." James 1:12

What were the most difficult times that God helped you through, Naomi?

There were several difficult months that were difficult, like seeing my EH (earthly husband) talking on the phone with OW (other woman), and also the trip he took with her that I believed was the end. Because when he returned, I saw a commitment ring on his finger from her instead of his wedding ring.

Every year we would take my mother-in-law to her sister's house so we could all vacation together. I went in the car with my sister-in-law and then my EH (earthly husband) said he was not going. It was when we arrived that we saw he had come and brought the OW (other woman) on vacation. That seemed like the end as everyone was shocked and thought I was going to physically attack them both. But by this time the contentious woman was gone and His love had given me a gentle and quiet spirit. I'd just finished Finding the Abundant Life and was on the next book about Living that life, on Chapter 4 "When Do I Give Up?" and I knew God allowed this for the testimony.

So I raised my head, walked over (which is when everyone believed I was going to attack her and him) and while walking...I repeated in my heart, "Fear nothing, God is with you." "If God is for me, who can be against me" and trusted what He wanted to do. I instead said, "Hi my name is Naomi, you must be... (saying her name)" and hugged her.

Naomi, what was the "turning point" of your restoration?

The turning point was when I decided to put into practice everything I learned at RMI, I'd passed the test when facing the OW (other woman) as I felt her shudder when I hugged her and knew she felt His love, not my fear.

After that, I was able to treat my EH (earthly husband) with meekness, without looking at the situation anymore. Many told me to get rid of him but I didn't, I decided to follow God's advice as I was done with how the world had led me to the pit I'd fallen into. My EH (earthly husband)never left the house as I've said, and I never stopped sleeping with him, just as it is in 1Corinthians 7:4, which clearly says: "The wife does not have authority over her own body, but the husband does; and likewise the husband also does not have authority over his own body, but the wife does."

Tell us HOW it happened, Naomi? Did your husband just walk in the front door? Naomi, did you suspect or could you tell you were close to being restored?

I started to pray through the book of Hosea, which talks about the hedge of thorns, building a spiritual fence around him. So when it was my

EH's birthday I asked God if it was His will that my husband would choose to spend his birthday with us, and that's what God did. I was home alone when I heard a car coming up our driveway and looked out to see, it was my EH (earthly husband). I was shocked. Even those who have FAITH are amazed by the works of God. When I opened the door, he came in and was carrying food and snacks. Then he went back to his car and immediately began to remove everything from the car that had been at OW's house. That day he didn't say what happened and I didn't ask, I just praised Him with such joy as I'd never known. I immediately began to prepare dinner for him that day and the next day, his birthday, we celebrated my EH (earthly husband) "officially" returning home. His heart was home with me and his family once again.

We are now in the post-restoration phase, as it is not over yet like most of the testimonies I read in the series of testimony books I studied, so I was prepared. I had not sent in my RMT because I believed it may not be restored because the day I began writing it, something was said by my EH (earthly husband), so I became confused. I do apologize for that, it was when I read a praise report talking about how this is the enemy's way of stealing God's praise and I instantly knew, that yes, God had already restored my marriage and how could I fail not to testify what GOD had done.

My EH (earthly husband) says he loves me, that all our difficulties are ending and we are currently making plans to finish our house and move in. Glory to God. He says that he only feels pleasure with me and that when he was with the OW (other woman) it was me that he longed for. What more proof does anyone need to see what God has done?

Would you recommend any of our resources in particular that helped you, Naomi?

I went through several trials but nothing kept me from the love of God, because I knew that He would be there and that He would perform His miracle. But I confess that I could not have done it alone, without the RMI materials I would never have known God's promises nor the love of my HH (Heavenly Husband). I recommend all the many courses you provide and am amazed how so few don't take advantage of what's offered. I tackled your courses even more than I had done when at university. I knew what I was learning would mean eternal rewards, not temporary and would reach far into every area of my life.

Would you be interested in helping encourage other women, Naomi?

Yes

Either way, Naomi, what kind of encouragement would you like to leave women with, in conclusion?

Your family is God's favorite project, and God's project makes no mistakes in how He does everything. No matter what you face, even should you face the enemy, remember the battle is in the mind and heart. Never look at the situation just for itself but the intent of Him allowing it. He is faithful and does nothing in half. God chose you to be the heart of your family, so fight for it as our Savior fought for us. He trusted God His Father and so must we. So my sisters, whatever happens, move forward and literally embrace and don't reject evil, because that evil can be quenched by His love. Trust me because I am living proof of what God can do.

Chapter 32

Ellen

"Therefore let us draw near with confidence
to the throne of grace, so that we may receive
mercy and find grace to help in time of need."
—Hebrews 4:16

"Involved with an OM and God Had Mercy on Me"

Ellen, how did your Restoration Journey actually begin?

It all started very early in my marriage, when I found in my EH's wallet there was a letter in which he said that he still loved his ex-girlfriend and that he regretted not being with her. It was a very difficult moment but as I was raised in the church and had already participated in some seminars for marriage, I forgave my husband and was determined that I would help him to forget her and that I would be beside him in spite of everything.

After this episode of betrayal, there were several others. I searched for and discovered his cell phone passwords, social media (like a good "wife" was advised to do by all her friends and even "experts") and discovered several conversations with other women and saw how bad he talked about our marriage to everyone. Even then I stayed because I loved him so much and I always believed that marriage is forever.

After 3 years of marriage, things got much worse, my EH (earthly husband) said he didn't love me anymore, that he didn't want me anymore and that he wanted to separate. He tried several times but I wouldn't let him leave me. I cried a lot, begged him to stay, called several pastors to convince him to stay and he ended up staying but the situation got even worse. He started to get involved with "friends" from the church he attended and came home at dawn. He never paid attention to me and he always insisted on telling me that he didn't want to be with me, that he was with me because I was forcing him to stay and I really was. I was a Pharisee.

I only lived in the church and whenever he wanted to do something (which was very rare) I said I couldn't because I had something going on at the church, so he went alone but I was sure I was doing the right thing, after all I was at church. What a fool I was! Shortly after this, he told me he had decided that we would break up and nothing that I did or say would make it stay.

Once again I cried and begged but he said he would only wait a few days and then would leave me forever. On Halloween, I arrived back from college (yes, pursuing a college degree as I tore my own house down, a warning to all you out there) and when I got home, his things were no longer there. But this time I was different, without crying and without despair, I texted him that when he left I would close the door on us. I said I was at peace and went to sleep.

The next day, I got up, opened my laptop and began looking for something on the internet to learn about restored marriages. If it was even possible and the next thing I knew God brought me here! I started reading everything offered. I dug into your courses like I was taking a college course (and weeks later I dropped out because I realized I was hungry for His Word and His truth. What else really mattered?) I simply couldn't stop reading each and everything. I also immediately started putting the principles into practice.

A week later, I found out about OW (other woman) who was one of his "friends" at church and it brought with it immense pain. I spent 30 days feeling unbearable pain in my chest, it was the worst thing I've ever felt. Once again I cried and begged for my husband to come back to me, but he said he would only stay a few days and leave me again. Is that what I wanted? I realized I couldn't do it in the flesh, I needed to put my trust and heart in His care.

How did God change your situation, Ellen, as you sought Him wholeheartedly?

I practiced letting go, I decided I didn't care, I didn't look, I didn't send messages, nor did I ask for help from him in anything. Despite being alone with my son, paying rent and being unemployed. I finally left him free to live however he wanted to live and trust that if it was His plan, God would turn his heart back to me. I literally disappeared from him. Off of social media, I was gone for good. And that's when God started to act. One night I was alone at home and he called me. I am glad I answered because I hadn't answered his calls or texts. I was told by a friend that he was traveling that day, so when I answered the phone he asked me to open the door saying he was home and just parking the car. He came in, we talked for a while and we were intimate. I remember that he repeated several times that I was different, that I had changed a lot and was I involved with anyone. I felt led not to answer. I just smiled and said nothing.

What principles, from God's Word (or through our resources), Ellen, did the Lord teach you during this trial?

The principles that helped me the most were letting go, being quiet (disappearing gave him time to both heal and think about me) and winning without words. Each was fundamental since he often called me just to get nasty with me and it hurt me a lot. So disappearing was clearly God's plan to help me heal as well.

What were the most difficult times that God helped you through, Ellen?

The most difficult moment was when I found out about OW (other woman) mainly because I knew her because she lives on the same street that we used to live on. After we got back together, he invited me to live with him at my mother-in-law's house, since I was unable to pay the rent. This phase was also very hard in my journey because it was horrible to be in the same house as him knowing that he was dating and yet he came to me for intimacy and promised to end the relationship. I was ridiculed, humiliated by his family and mine for accepting that situation. But God honored me and removed her from his mind and heart.

Ellen, what was the "turning point" of your restoration?

The turning point was when God changed everything in my favor even though I didn't deserve it. I say this because I was weak. I fell into the enemy's trap and ended up getting involved with an OM (other man), a guy from a company where I once worked for. Even in this situation God had mercy on me and forgave me. When EH (earthly husband) found out I had been involved with someone else, he went into total despair and started chasing me. (I want to make it clear that I am not proud of it, in fact I am ashamed to talk about it, because I set a bad example but God does things as he wants). The shame that wants to envelop me now is simply not worth it. The only good is that I am able to see the shame husbands may come home with and why they act the way they do.

Tell us HOW it happened, Ellen? Did your husband just walk in the front door? Ellen, did you suspect or could you tell you were close to being restored?

My EH (earthly husband) started sending me messages saying that he loved me, that I was the woman of his life and that he couldn't exist without me. I never replied but I didn't block him either. He came to talk to me and said he wanted our marriage back but I still said nothing in reply. He sent messages to my friends asking them for help to get the "woman of his dreams" back. He asked me for forgiveness for all the mistakes he made and asked me to start over, fresh, from scratch.

Our HH (Heavenly Husband) is really beautiful. Who knew things would change so much?! Today we are together and building our home. My EH (earthly husband) says daily that he loves me and several times I've caught him just staring at me, loving me. We must do our part nevertheless it is God who has taken care of this restoration. I am a deep sinner who is unworthy. Thank you, Lord!

Would you recommend any of our resources in particular that helped you, Ellen?

Yes. I recommend the book "How God can and will restore your marriage" to start, take the courses and watch the videos as each was instrumental in my journey.

Would you be interested in helping encourage other women, Ellen?

Yes of course!

Either way, Ellen, what kind of encouragement would you like to leave women with, in conclusion?

My loved ones, do not give up! No matter what the situation is, no matter how humiliated and ridiculed you have been. Even if you fall into the pit of sin as I did. God is going to perform a miracle for you if you trust Him "Stand and watch the salvation of your marriage. But you will not even need to fight. Take your positions; then stand still and watch the Lord's victory. He is with you, O people of Judah and Jerusalem. Do not be afraid or discouraged. Go out against them tomorrow, for the Lord is with you!" 2 Chronicles 20:17

Chapter 33

Candace

"My Beloved is mine, and I am His"
—Song of Solomon 2:16

"My Marriage was Restored in Exactly 90 Days THIS Time"

Candace, how did your Restoration Journey actually begin?

After the Lord had already blessed me with a restored marriage, I abandoned my Heavenly Husband again, and once again I was a fool and allowed the enemy to enter my house, he came to steal, kill and destroy, but the Lord came here for everyone to have life and live it abundantly. So I ran back to my Abundant Life courses, repeating You're all I want my Love, You're all I need my Darling, You're all I promise to Live for!

But I knew I needed more, so I read A Wise Woman because this shows us how to live restored and started taking it as a course. Today I finished course 3. Beloved ones, don't miss taking the courses, and journaling your heart because it was very important for my journey to restore both times! I learned many things that I couldn't even imagine. Each time I took them, each time I journaled, I could see how much I was growing spiritually and my life got better. All the Glory goes to my Beloved who did not abandon me and welcomed me with all his love, drenching me in it even after I failed and began focusing on pleasing my husband (which caused him to loathe me rather than pursue me like he did when I was only interested in my HH (Heavenly Husband)), then decided to give me another chance for the sake of my children to have their father living and married to their mom. "Darling, I am so grateful you once again restored me to You and then restored my marriage." "My Beloved is mine, and I am His" Song of Solomon 2:16

How did God change your situation, Candace, as you sought Him wholeheartedly?

I went searching for my Lord more and more, with all my heart! I woke up earlier and earlier in the morning to have time alone with Him. Also to kill my flesh, I did a lot of fasting, and even without eating I felt very good because I was fed with His word, and every day I felt stronger and stronger in my faith and even more, I felt His presence right by my side. I no longer sang songs of praise about Him, but now together we have a song of our own, a love song!

When I woke up in the morning I was so thankful that He was giving me another day to be in love with Him. I can no longer leave my house or start my day without thanking Him with tears in my eyes for all the wonders that He does in my life. Each day I would feel more and more loved, more intimate with Him, and each time I looked for him, the more my EH (earthly husband) began wanting me and realized the greatest changes my EH (earthly husband) made in his life were times I was most in love with my HH (Heavenly Husband)) just as Erin and all the ministers say. It's true. It's all true and my life and story confirms it.

What principles, from God's Word (or through our resources), Candace, did the Lord teach you during this trial?

That I have to be obedient to the Lord, follow His word, be submissive to my husband, but most importantly is that my HH (Heavenly Husband) is first and no one else. It also was very important to let go of my husband and the church (I began to falter in this as well), to win without words, to resist the enemy and my flesh, to pray without ceasing, to fast, to give the tithe (Beloved if you are not tithing to the house where you are fed, do this as quickly as possible, it's essential. You have no idea how easily the enemy will continue to steal from you because you gave him permission to.), I give my tithe to this ministry, my house, because this ministry feeds me daily, and when I am not here I literally starve spiritually. The church is junk food and does nothing to make us want more of Him.

Be sure to Praise the Lord in good and bad times, because some of the sweetest times were when we walked together in the valleys of the shadow of death, I feared no harm, for the Lord was with me, and He cuddled with me and sometimes carried me in His arms, He held me, protected me under his wings.

What were the most difficult times that God helped you through, Candace?

Because I was an adulteress, my husband attacked me with ghastly words. He said that he did not want me anymore, that he did not love me, but while my husband spoke, I only thought about the Lord and spoke to and listened to Him. I knew that He was with me and told me that it was all a lie that my husband was saying to me, that he was being a slave to the enemy, so soon my husband would calm down and hug me as I remained silent and praised Him in the midst. He'd apologize and say to me: "I don't know why I fight with you anymore, I try to do everything to provoke you, but I see that nothing hits you or hurts you. I don't know why I am doing this to you." Other times that were difficult is that my husband had clothes at home and some at his parents' house, and when he didn't sleep at home, my daughter would cry and keep asking why her dad wouldn't come back, and my son would just sulk and become anti-social. So I would ask my HH (Heavenly Husband) to be with us and lie down in bed in the place where my husband slept, to calm my daughter, and to be the Heavenly Father to my son and talk with him, giving his little heart wisdom and comfort.

Candace, what was the "turning point" of your restoration?

When I handed everything over to the Lord, and once again, He was all I wanted, needed and lived for. I knew that my marriage would be restored for the sake of my children (I was fine living as His bride but my children were hurting). It's also true that God hates divorce, and this time divorce was threatened so I read both divorce books and loved when Michele said to be enthusiastic because once that was my attitude rather than fear my EH (earthly husband) dropped from ever uttering those words to me). Even if this time my restoration was years later, I knew it was going to happen at His appointed time. His will was always done in my life only because I trusted Him with all my heart. Oh, after I let go, this time I started to encourage other women and in an instant everything changed. This also works like everyone says.

Tell us HOW it happened, Candace? Did your husband just walk in the front door? Candace, did you suspect or could you tell you were close to being restored?

This time my husband only took a few things to his mother's (and God told me why He had to remove lover and friend because I'd become an adulteress and left my first love.

Glory to God, so my loved ones, when your marriages are restored do not forget to send your testimony and continue to be obedient to the Lord, keep Him in first place. Don't force God to remove him from your house and hurt your children or yourself. Because I was the fool and I abandoned my first love again, the Lord lovingly brought me back to Him again to show me that I have to be obedient to His Word and no longer be an adulteress.

Today I am His and He is mine, He is wonderful. This time I could hear Him so clearly when we talked together and one day it happened at my lunchtime break. I don't know why I asked but I said, when will my marriage be restored? I heard very soon.

The next morning when I woke up, I was on my computer taking my Poverty Mentality course and when he got up he gave me a hug (because he had been sleeping at home for almost a month on the couch) and he asked me if I would go with him to his mother's to get all his things. My heart began pounding but I just looked at him and said calmingly yes, of course. Ladies, I just have to praise and thank Him, for everything He does in my life. I know that His work in me will never be complete.

My marriage was restored in exactly 90 days this time because I knew just what to do and didn't fool around with doubt. I was able to praise in all the bad times and focus on my HH (Heavenly Husband). I just have to praise and thank my Lord. I couldn't believe it, my Lord gave me the answer the night before it happened because of our intimacy. I am in awe.

Would you recommend any of our resources in particular that helped you, Candace?

I would recommend to everyone: First the book RYM, which was very important to start the journey, then A Wise Woman (don't miss this course), Praise that Sets us Free, also Hinds Feet in High Places I recommend that everyone read (or listen to as there's an audiobook that's wonderful). Also, wake up early and read the Encourager every day, then the daily devotionals. Also if you are listening to the wrong voices, listen to Erin by watching the Be encouraged videos I always felt encouraged and the testimonies that I reread whenever I began doubting. I bought the series of e-books.

Would you be interested in helping encourage other women, Candace?

Certainly, it will be a great pleasure to encourage other women. I already meet with women every week to study a wise woman.

Either way, Candace, what kind of encouragement would you like to leave women with, in conclusion?

Beloved friend, never give up on your marriages, the Lord does not want to see any family separated, He hates divorce. Like streams of water like this is the heart of the king in the hand of the Lord, who inclines him to all his will. God is wonderful, He never leaves His bride. He just wants you to Himself, that's why you're here, for no other reason. Trust me, I made this journey twice. I also want to take this time to thank Erin for creating the ministry and being willing to encourage so many women no matter how many times she got attacked. I pray that God blesses you and your entire family and the ministers here.

Chapter 34

Eunice

"So, as those who have been chosen of God,
holy and beloved, put on a heart of compassion,
kindness, humility, gentleness and patience."
—Colossians 3:12

"I Saw Him Looking at Me with a Silly Passionate Look"

Eunice, how did your Restoration Journey actually begin?

Well, this story is a little long. My husband and I met in our teens and I soon fell in love with him and he then started showing interest in me and we started dating. In the following years we became engaged and got married. We were always very good friends and enjoyed being with each other (which made our situation very difficult when we were separated). It was just years ago when my husband and I were fighting a lot. I was like many of the women who are disgustingly contentious and everything had to be my way. Then one day I saw my husband crying and when I asked him what happened, thinking someone had died or something, he told me that there was an OW (other woman) and that he was going to leave me. I couldn't believe it. Never in a million years would I ever believe that he would do that. I tried to get help from my parents (who came to talk to us), get help from our favorite pastor of our church, I tried to talk with my husband, but none of that helped, he left home, taking all his things with him.

I didn't know about RMI, but I always believed in God and His Word (although I didn't read it often and had no clue about any principles for marriage or wives) but in my heart I knew that He had a purpose in all this and that He didn't want my marriage to be destroyed. So I soon had a peace in my heart and I started to seek Him and believe in what He could do. I started to follow some principles that I already knew. A friend had a restored marriage, so I know you had to be meek and kind whenever I had the opportunity to talk to my husband, to be sweet with every word spoken and to not judge him for anything that had happened. God was giving me wisdom and grace to endure everything.

Then my husband started to approach me again. There was one time that he even called me crying saying that he missed me, but that he didn't know how to get out of his mess and if he came back if we would be successful, that he had complicated his whole life and it was hopeless. Then on the internet I found the book How God can and will restore your marriage and I started to read it. In less than a week I had read the whole book 3 times and started to practice everything I had learned.

So I made a vow with the Lord and every day for 7 days I would get up at dawn to pray for my husband, not for our marriage, but for his salvation and for God to deliver him as he had told me was how he felt. And then, exactly on the last day of my prayer, my husband returned home, after almost 2 months away from home. He returned broken, but happy, saying that he loved me and wanted to live with me forever.

We resumed our work in the church. We were part of the ministry of praise and several times we gave our testimonies in the church and so this was our first restoration.

Fast forward to 3 years later. Exactly in the same way as the first time, we were experiencing a crisis in our marriage. I was unemployed for almost a year and I became contentious because I could not help my husband and I failed to trust God. We discussed things like our time at church that occupied our time almost every weekend (which was the time we had together, since in the week he worked a lot) and then I stopped practicing everything I had learned at RMI and turned away from the Lord.

Then, my husband left me and when I realized he'd moved out, I remembered everything I had learned and everything we had been through before. I searched boxes and found the book How God Can and Will Restore Your Marriage and I started reading it again and practicing the principles. I repented for leaving it behind and turning away from the Lord. I prayed and asked Him to take me back. And then I started to act differently, but still with God's permission, my husband continued living elsewhere but not with the OW (other woman). Instead, he went to live with his mother.

It was hard to see him go, but I knew the Word, I knew what I'd done and I knew that with him there I would fail again to follow the principles. Mainly I knew that the Lord was trying to bring me back to Him again and finally, even with all this happening, I was able to be at peace.

I began to yearn for the Lord more than ever and finally I got to know the RMI website and all it had to offer. So I started taking the courses, and what a difference, with each lesson I was learning more and more and being set free from myself while wanting more and more of the Lord. I was changing so much I was amazed. My journals became love letters to Him. And then I was finally able to have a relationship with Him as I never had, I finally met Him as my Beloved, my HH (Heavenly Husband), my protector and provider and that was so wonderful I just can't describe it.

I learned to let go because He was everything I needed. It was so easy because I had so much of Him. I never could have imagined my life would be so beautiful.

If my husband spoke too ugly to me, I was all right. If he did not speak for weeks, I no longer suffered because I was happy to be alone with Him and because I knew that He was taking care of everything and that everything was in His control. I loved getting home and lying in bed and singing new love songs to Him that I'd heard on the radio. I loved talking to Him, feeling His embrace and feeling that He was with me all the time. When I went to work (I got a job just before my husband left the house, and I started to work because my husband asked me, though I prayed against it) when looking at the sun rising while on the train, I could see my Beloved in everything, I could see Him as the center of everything in my life. I loved spending every moment with Him and I knew that He would never forsake me. He would never turn His back on me and never gave up on me.

So when I was at the height of my relationship with Him, my Beloved, my Lover, when I learned that He is my Husband and that I am His bride and that I look forward to being able to see Him and embrace Him and be with Him, my EH (earthly husband) started to get closer to me, to say that he loved me, but I was afraid for him to come back and make the mistakes again. I also didn't want to lose what I had with my Beloved.

I listened to him, asking me to please get back together again but I didn't speak much. I was in no hurry to have him at home. I was even afraid to get too far away from my HH (Heavenly Husband) and not have the quality time that we now had. But I left everything in His hands and rested saying that I knew that if He wanted it, I would willingly allow Him to restore my marriage, but that He had to promise that nothing would change between us. I wanted everything to stay the way we had it. So I prayed and said Your will be done.

It was very crazy how so many things that I read in the courses confirmed how I was feeling. That my restoration was ripe to pick when I no longer wanted it and I only wanted Him. By this time I wasn't on any social networks and then I read the lesson talking about leaving the church, and after several confirmations, even though it seems crazy, I let my church go and that's when everything changed.

How did God change your situation, Eunice, as you sought Him wholeheartedly?

Showing me every day where He wanted to transform me, showing me how He wanted to approach me and be intimate and close to Him, to show Him that He is all I need. Every day I came home and ran to get ready and go to "our little corner of our world" where I could talk to Him, sing to Him, feel Him and that changed me. Every day I just wanted to be better for Him, because He loved me, took care of me, supplied me with everything and gave me a peace that I cannot explain.

What principles, from God's Word (or through our resources), Eunice, did the Lord teach you during this trial?

There were so many I could never list them all. But the ones that helped me the most in this RJ were speaking kindness everytime we speak, gentle and quiet spirit, letting go, letting the church go, putting the Lord always first in everything in my life, trusting only Him and His word.

What were the most difficult times that God helped you through, Eunice?

When my husband left home, I saw him (on social media), where one of his ex-girlfriends from high school was also in and they were laughing and hugging. It was very difficult because the enemy wanted to put several thoughts in my mind and so I cried so much at the Lord's feet. I'm so thankful to Him for using it to allure me back to Him, to His ways. Without Him I would not have succeeded.

Eunice, what was the "turning point" of your restoration?

First when I understood to let you go. I realized that letting go is not just not getting in touch and leaving him alone, but leaving your heart free from wanting him and proof when you no longer want to know what is going on, how restoration will happen or when it will happen. Letting go is "not" caring about time, distance, attitudes, it is resting in God and dedicating yourself and focusing on seeking Him and giving Him your whole heart and receiving everything He wants to give you (good and bad), and allowing yourself to enjoy His sweet presence and receive a love that you will never find in your life and the only way to be truly happy, because your happiness is in Him.

Tell us HOW it happened, Eunice? Did your husband just walk in the front door? Eunice, did you suspect or could you tell you were close to being restored?

For a couple of weeks he started visiting me, calling me, talking to me more when I did answer. Then he started saying that he missed me and he started talking about coming back and if I believed it could work. Then one day he met me at home and said he wanted to come back, that he felt such a peace when he was with me, that he loved me and missed me a lot, that his heart was hurting so much he couldn't stand it. He asked me to go to see a movie, we met there and when we went inside, during the entire movie, he started whispering all these loving words into my ear. I saw him looking at me with a silly passionate look and started saying he had to come back to where he never should have left and said he would do anything for us. Then he thanked me for not giving up on us. That same day, after the movie, we went home together and the next day he moved his things back in.

Would you recommend any of our resources in particular that helped you, Eunice?

Yes, the book How God can and will restore your marriage helped me a lot. It helped me in the direction I knew I needed to go and showed me the light at the end of the tunnel. I recommend the courses, what a difference than just reading the book (which I intend to continue doing, as our RJ does not end and should not end) and the book A Wise Woman. These materials helped me soooo much, you have no idea and that's why I recommend and share them with people I know have been through the same things that I went through and also shared with friends who are getting married. I would have loved to have all this information before you got married.

Would you be interested in helping encourage other women, Eunice?

Yes, and I believe that the Lord allowed this to happen to me so that I could get closer and get to know Him and then help others who are going through the same situation and help prevent young women from making the same mistakes.

Either way, Eunice, what kind of encouragement would you like to leave women with, in conclusion?

Well, I went through what you are going through and I know how difficult it is, but I have good news, you don't have to suffer. There is a path of peace, a path of joy and happiness in the midst of all that suffering dear friend. You can have peace, and this path begins by falling in love with your Maker.

Dear ones, don't focus on your husband, don't focus on your marriage, focus on Him and His will. Desire to know Him, to want to please Him, to want to feel everything He wants to offer you. Oh it is so wonderful, so beautiful and such a unique experience you do not want to miss.

Today only He makes my heart race, only He fills my eyes with tears of emotion, He is everything you need and He allowed this to happen so that you could return to Him. He has so much to offer you, more than any man in this world could ever hope to give you. Take advantage of this time, every second of it to be with your Beloved, really try to know Him and you will never be the same. Enjoy every moment because soon God will restore your marriage and you will not have all the time you have today to be with Him.

Do not give up what He said you would do, do not give up on His promises and the testimony He has through your life and marriage. And please never forget that He is in control of everything and that for Him nothing is impossible. I love you even without knowing you, and I wish with all my heart that you enjoy Him and if you do, very soon you will have the blessing of a restored marriage and you'll be writing your own testimony.

Chapter 35

Lydia

"Behold, children are a gift of the Lord;
the fruit of the womb is a reward."
—Psalm 127:3

"He Suspected the Baby was Not His"

Lydia, how did your Restoration Journey actually begin?

Well, we met, dated, got engaged and I got pregnant. So we got married. He was my first boyfriend and the first I was ever intimate with. I have always been very jealous, and the enemy has always used this to control my life. I began hearing rumors about my husband, saying he was betraying me, which at the time was not true, but whenever I heard something, I remember fighting and accusing him without giving him a chance to say a word in his defense or set me right. So with that going on, I was always suspicious of everything he told me he was going to do. I was a nightmare, to be honest. I would interrogate him before he left to know where he was going, what he was doing and then did the same when he came back.

Besides living through this, during our fights I was unbearable. I wanted to have the last word. I said things that attacked his manhood and just him as a person. Often I'd get to the point of becoming aggressive. And whenever we fought, he said things from the past. For example, remember that day when..... and the fight became more intense, screaming so loud for everyone in the building to hear.

The fights over time became worse and the suspicion increased due to my EH (earthly husband) working at night for extra money as an Uber driver. Besides the comments about him cheating on me were increasing and with more details. In one discussion I remember I told him if he was not happy, take his things and leave. This happened when he'd come home at noon after getting off late in the morning. But until then I didn't know that there was an OW (other woman), which came much later, many months after I began accusing him (and later he told me he said he might as well cheat since I accused him). After I kicked him out is when he hooked up with the first one. Friends never tell your husband to get out or accuse them of cheating because you are just as much at fault. You will regret it and when you ask them to return, they won't. This is what I did and how all of this happened. I asked if there was another woman but he denied it and I couldn't understand why he didn't come back.

We owned a small coffee bar that I was supposed to take care of, but in my arrogance and stupidity I didn't want to take care of it anymore and told him so. It was then that he hired a girl to look after the store and later I discovered it was his new girlfriend.

I discovered this when some relatives came to get coffee and seeing her showed me pictures of him on a trip with the two of them she'd posted on Facebook.

It was terrible because at the same time I called him saying a lot and telling him to get that woman out of there. The coffee bar was located a block from my house, where I lived with my daughter and auntie. This is where my most intense furnace began but it's where I met my Heavenly Husband who gradually transformed me. I always wanted the restoration of my marriage, and that's when I started to search on the Internet to find out about it. I was directed by everyone to the RMI. As I read the book [How God Can and Will Restore Your Marriage], I realized how wrong I was, how contentious, arrogant and impatient I was.

A week later I took the first of a dozen of your courses and applied them to my life. Gradually everyone started to see my transformation. Even my EH (earthly husband) noticed and was puzzled.

It was a long journey to kill my flesh and act as our Beloved tells us to do to please Him and to find true peace and happiness. It wasn't easy at all. And I confess that sometimes I wanted my Beloved to make an exception just so that I didn't need to obey Him in something specific that hurt me a lot.

I learned a lot and am grateful for the time in the desert that I spent. Just the two of us. My Beloved and me. People find it strange when I say that. But I really feel grateful, because today I can be different and help the women around me not to act in ways that they later regret.

When reading the book [How God Can and Will Restore Your Marriage] a woman knew about Erin as a result of her having a baby after she'd determined she would have no more children. I knew that I needed to stop taking contraceptives, but since my EH (earthly husband) told me to take them, I submitted but I longed to have more children again. Then one day in my bathroom I fervently prayed to my HH (Heavenly Husband) and I told Him that I gave Him my womb and my whole body and my family, leaving everything into His hands. I'd always wanted a son and often my daughter asked me for a baby brother and every time she asked me for this I told her to pray and we would trust our Heavenly Father for His perfect plan. Only He could give us this tremendous blessing.

So at the end of the year, my EH (earthly husband) spent it with us just as I'd asked my HH (Heavenly Husband) for. I continued to take the pill as usual and was submissive to my EH (earthly husband) but my longing for a child increased. Then in March I found out I was two months pregnant. It was a bit scary because my EH (earthly husband) was not with us. So, again I cried to Him because I didn't really want it to be that way and told Him I just trusted in His power and He was so merciful that He answered my every request.

As of today it's been four and a half months since my EH (earthly husband) came back, enjoying our new baby boy and being a family again. My EH (earthly husband) told me that he chose to take care of his family after seeing the incredible change in me. When he told me I restrained myself but wanted to shout "All Glory to God!!!" because if it were not for Him, nothing that I am living today would have been possible. He is faithful and I believe in Him and will never doubt Him again in anything!

How did God change your situation, Lydia, as you sought Him wholeheartedly?

My Beloved has transformed me from the inside. He healed me of my childhood wounds and traumas, gave me enormous security due to His love for me. What was fundamental is my self-worth as being His, not in self-esteem or self-love but His love. All that garbage is what created the unbearable contentious woman who I am so thankful is gone. He taught me His principles with every step I took, showered in His love.

What principles, from God's Word (or through our resources), Lydia, did the Lord teach you during this trial?

I learned several principles. First was to put your Heavenly Husband first and as proof, no matter what, be submissive to my husband, to trust God without hesitation. They were the main ones that helped me not to go back to the old me.

What were the most difficult times that God helped you through, Lydia?

The most difficult times were when my EH (earthly husband) came and went and my daughter was crying a lot. It killed me inside because I'd known I was at fault. But I always tried to follow what Erin says. I trusted in a way that I can't explain. And I always cried out to Him especially when I thought I was going to sink and He gave me His hand and lifted me up.

Lydia, what was the "turning point" of your restoration?

Well I believe it was a day that my EH (earthly husband) saw each other by chance after several months of letting go. He'd taken the OW (other woman) to live with him again and my daughter found out through a cousin. I already knew, but I didn't say anything. I just trusted my HH (Heavenly Husband). At about this time my Beloved embraced me one difficult day and told me "it has already ended, get ready for his return." So in my heart I had the feeling that there would be a test.

My daughter went to the coffee house (where he was working with the OW (other woman)) and asked him if it was true and so when my EH (earthly husband) saw me, he accused me of sending her to speak to him. I kept my cool and said that I already knew before she knew and that I had no reason to say anything to her, not wanting to hurt her or to cause her to dishonor him as her father. I told him not to worry that I would talk to our daughter so she wouldn't act like that again and told him that she was following my bad example as a contentious woman, the kind of person I didn't want her to ever become. It was then that his attitude changed completely, and a day later, he called me saying he realized I'd changed but he'd never come back. I assured him he was free to do whatever made him happy and I didn't blame him at all. He said a few cutting remarks but I continued to treat him with great affection and love. Something I would never have achieved. Only my Beloved could transform a person like me like this.

It was then that we started to see each other more and more. He promised that he would come back, but I got pregnant and our final test came. He suspected the baby was not his, but I never had been with another man besides my husband, not ever in my whole life. I waited and waited patiently for God to defend me and Glory to Him, the Lord spoke to his heart assuring him it was his.

Tell us HOW it happened, Lydia? Did your husband just walk in the front door? Lydia, did you suspect or could you tell you were close to being restored?

As I said, he made several promises that he would return and that's what happened. I had a doctor's appointment for an ultrasound close to where he lived and he said he wanted to come. So he came and we went home together. Hallelujah. The next day he moved his things home.

Would you recommend any of our resources in particular that helped you, Lydia?

I recommend all the tools that Erin has given to us and are readily at our disposal. Especially the book [How God Can and Will Restore Your Marriage] every woman seems to find when searching for help.

Would you be interested in helping encourage other women, Lydia?

Yes

Either way, Lydia, what kind of encouragement would you like to leave women with, in conclusion?

Believe me dear friend, even if your thoughts and desires are to want to give up, in the midst of the daily struggles you have been through, you just have to believe. Our Beloved is wonderful and cannot lie. Share your heart with Him, speak His Word as His promises to you and really believe that what He puts in your heart will be the outcome of your journey. Don't throw it all away due to emotions and lies. Run to Him. Dear friend, don't give up because it will be worth it and these days will be the best of your life!

Chapter 36

Bethany

"Be strong and courageous, and do the work. Do not be afraid or
discouraged, for the Lord God, my God, is with you."
—1 Chronicles 28:20

"Restored on My Birthday"

Bethany, how did your Restoration Journey actually begin?

Friends, my ordeal started in February. One Saturday my husband said
he was going to have lunch with some friends, when he returned later
he was distant, and he barely spoke to me. At night I asked if something
had happened, and he replied that he was tired of the relationship and
that he had not been happy for a long time. He told me that he wanted
to end our 5-year marriage ... I cried, begged, asked what had happened
and as I came near him, he just didn't want me to touch him anymore,
as if he disgusted me! He said that for him there was no reason for us
to continue together.

On Sunday I tried to talk to him again, Lord ... how I was wrong
insisting! I asked him for a chance, but he said he didn't like me
anymore. But after that, for 1 month it looked like he was trying to stay
in the marriage ... in the month of April, 2 months later, he texted me
from his cell phone and said that I knew what he wanted, and I was
reading the book "How God can and will restore your marriage." I cried
so much when I read the "contentious woman" chapter, I saw all my
mistakes just like I was watching a movie. I asked God to forgive me,
and He welcomed me back to be close to Him ... Praise be to God!!!

Meanwhile, my husband had not left the house, so at the end of April,
he said he wanted to talk, he said that it was no longer good for him to
be with me, that our relationship was never good, only at the very
beginning, and that whenever he wanted to separate, I didn't let him,
not when we were in courtship nor during our marriage. That hurt too
much, but I didn't cry, I held on just listening. Then I told him if it is
not good for us to be together and he wanted to take a break, he was

free to leave in order to think. And I said I was going to go for a walk so he could decide. Before I left, he said he had one more thing ... that he likes another woman. I sat down again and asked how long ago, and he said since the end of the previous year, so for almost five months! That day he decided to leave, but I'm thankful because he left only once. I remained firm in the Lord, because He was holding me, I didn't cry, I didn't despair! Our God guided me and helped me in this humiliating hour that I never imagined I'd ever face.

How did God change your situation, Bethany, as you sought Him wholeheartedly?

Since I found the site HopeAtLast.com, began reading the testimonies and then the RYM book, I started to see the mistakes I made in my life. That God was really calling me to become a better person, it wasn't just about my marriage. The truth was everything irritated me, everything, however small, was capable of destabilizing me. Then I screamed, I fought, I argued ... I was really the epitome of a contentious woman that no one could take being around.

My EH left home at the beginning of May, and before he left, he said emphatically "it's over for me, there's no going back."

What principles, from God's Word (or through our resources), Bethany, did the Lord teach you during this trial?

I learned a lot by reading the book How God Can and Will Restore Your Marriage. I asked God to always strengthen my faith, I asked Him to show me what it was like to be content because I couldn't understand it! Friends, He put me in situations and made me feel content, I couldn't believe it! I thank Him so much for showing me what such contentment is!!! I started to sleep better and when I lay down I talked to Him and asked Him to hug me and take care of me while I sleep! When I wake up I say, "Good morning my Love" to Him and when I get out of bed I am talking to Him as I begin my day and all day long until I close my eyes at night.

The Lord said to have faith, be strong and have courage and trust Him, that only He could help me!! God lit my way!!! I love you my Darling from today to eternity!!!

What were the most difficult times that God helped you through, Bethany?

The most difficult times were when my EH left home, and when he suddenly appeared back at home, and promptly when he left again. God always guided me and was always showing me what to do, to say, to write, to think. Showing me this was a spiritual battle only He could fight on my behalf and my job was to let Him do it and fall head over heels for Him.

Bethany, what was the "turning point" of your restoration?

When I started asking God to do His will and not mine, after reading a lot about Letting go, God gave me a sense of peace and I was able to wait on Him. I even asked Him if it wasn't His will to restore, then I would be happy, really happy. About a week before my birthday I felt led to ask Him that on my birthday I would not like to feel sad, that I wanted to celebrate just with Him. I told Him that if my EH felt only pity and not love for me, then please let him not remember my birthday. Then I said the craziest thing, I asked the Lord that if it was His will, I would very much like my marriage to be restored on my birthday. But when I was saying it and even afterward I didn't want it restored. I was happier than I'd been in my life with just us two.

Tell us HOW it happened, Bethany? Did your husband just walk in the front door? Bethany, did you suspect or could you tell you were close to being restored?

On my birthday, he texted early and he invited me to dinner! Wow, I was floored. I wondered what it was all about but because I was at work and I was happy, with a heart at peace, I just didn't think about it anymore. That night we went to dinner, then he came home with me, and then asked if I would like to do something over the weekend. I said no, I'd rather not. Yes, my answer shocked me too! So then he asked me to go to his parent's house and I said I'd love to. We went together, and while we were alone, he apologized to me and hugged me! When we got home, he stayed and then the next morning he went to get his things from the place he was living! I couldn't believe it!! That was in May and it is now September!!! Forgive me everyone for not sharing my testimony sooner, forgive me Erin, but I kept doubting it was restored but how silly is that to think.

Would you recommend any of our resources in particular that helped you, Bethany?

The book How God Can and Will Restore, and the videos of Erin!! Erin gave me a lot of courage with her words of comfort! I am forever grateful, we both are! I did tell him about finding this ministry and he was in awe that anything like this could radically change someone so much as it changed me. I did tell him what I knew Erin would say, "it was God who changed me, they just gave me the roadmap to my journey." I smile when I think of it now.

Would you be interested in helping encourage other women, Bethany?

Yes

Either way, Bethany, what kind of encouragement would you like to leave women with, in conclusion?

Dear friend, have faith, believe that God and He alone can do this miracle! He fulfills our desires when we desire Him above all else and also that He does everything in His time, not ours. Everything you read here is in the Bible and it's true!!!!!!!!

What you have read is just a *small sample* of the POWER and FAITHFULNESS of God that are told through countless restored marriages! We continue to post new restored marriage, and restored relationship testimonies (children, siblings, parents, etc.) on our site each week.

Don't let ANYONE try to convince you that God cannot restore YOUR marriage! It is a lie. The TRUTH is that He is MORE THAN ABLE!!

Is Your Marriage... Crumbling? Hopeless? Or Ended in Divorce?

At Last There's Hope!

Have you been searching for marriage help online? It's not by chance, nor is it by coincidence, that you have this book in your hands. God is leading you to Restore Ministries that began by helping marriages that *appear* hopeless—like yours!

God has heard your cry for help in your marriage struggles and defeats. He predestined this **Divine Appointment** to give you the hope that you so desperately need right now!

We know and understand what you are going through since many of us in our restoration fellowship have a restored marriage and family! No matter what others have told you, your marriage is not hopeless! We know, after filling almost two books of restored marriage testimonies, that God is able to restore any marriage—especially yours!

"Behold, I am the LORD, the God of all flesh; is anything too difficult for Me?" (Jeremiah 32:27).

If you have been told that your marriage is hopeless or that without your husband's help your marriage cannot be restored! Each week we post a new Restored Relationship from one of our Restoration Fellowship Members that we post on our site.

"Ah Lord GOD! Behold, You have made the heavens and the earth by Your great power and by Your outstretched arm! Nothing is too difficult for You"! (Jeremiah 32:17).

If you have been crying out to God for more help, someone who understands, someone you can talk to, then we invite you to join our

RMI Restoration Fellowship. Since beginning this fellowship, we have seen more marriages restored on a regular basis than we ever thought possible!

Restoration Fellowship

Restoration is a "narrow road"—look around, most marriages end in divorce! But if your desire is for a restored marriage, then our Restoration Fellowship is designed especially for you!

Since beginning this fellowship, we have seen marriages restored more consistently than we ever thought possible.

Let us help you stay committed to "working with God" to restore your marriages. Restoration Fellowship can offer you the help, guidance, and support you will need to stay on the path that leads to victory—*your* marriage restored!

Let us assure you that all of our marriages were restored by GOD (through His Word) as we sought Him to lead us, teach us, guide us and transform us through His Holy Spirit. This, too, is all you need for *your* marriage to be restored.

However, God continues to lead people to our ministry and fellowship to gain the faith, support and help that so many say that they needed in their time of crisis.

"I want to thank each and every partner at this ministry for allowing me to access this wealth of knowledge and understanding of the word of God , while sharing all these testimonies of hope and love. This was a major encouragement to me while I am holding fast to God's word and His promises.

Even though I came across some of these principles before, the way it was dealt with left me with no confusion. I was lost to what I really had to do for the Lord and how He wanted me to do it but with you all I have been able to get a clearer vision of what is needed to increase my relationship with my Lord and Savior.

There is so much more I can say but thank you seems not to be enough.I look forward to learning so much more as these courses go along and I plan to do them over as many times as I can .

Please do the encouragement and the changes these wives experience is just an out pour of the goodness of God.

I was confused as to what I needed to do to grow my relationship with the Lord and while walking in faith for my marriage restoration. I sorted this site out in how I should do that. My husband and I were speaking but not as open and free as we are now after I have applied the principles to my life. I am seeing small changes in our communication. Praise God.

But I am focusing on my relationship with my HH (Heavenly Husband). No matter what the world throws at you, know that God is always with you and when you lean on Him He is always there to hold you up. He will find a way to reach you at your time of need all you have to do is hold in to His hand and seek His face." Farline in Trinidad and Tobago

"I would definitely recommend the RYM (Restore Your Marriage) book as a good resource and guide in navigating through your marital crises. This book always brings us back to the Bible and its biblical principles and reminding us that only God has the answers to our issues, not ourselves and not even our partners.

The testimonies have been powerful in reminding me that with God, all things are possible. I have been very inspired each time I read about how the Lord became the First Loves of the ladies who submitted their testimonies and how God swiftly restored their marriages and turned their earthly husbands' hearts back to them. These testimonies shows me that God wants and can restore our marriages if we focus our lives on Him alone. Thank you so much for sharing these wonderful testimonies and to God be the glory!

Before I found RMI, I kept ruminating about why the marriage had broken down and I was desperate to problem solve and trying to salvage the marriage. However, after reading the RYM [Restore Your Marriage] book, going through C1: Renew and through journaling, I got better insights into my role in the breakdown and how an abandonment is needed for the Lord to work on my life and draw me back into His loving arms.

I also realized that my earthly husband was my idol that I placed as priority that has led to the abandonment that is needed.

The resources shared have drawn me into closer intimacy with our Heavenly Husband and helps me find greater purposes for my life. Thank you so much for the resources that is much needed for those in similar situations." Lee in Singapore

Join our Restoration Fellowship TODAY and allow us to help YOU **restore** YOUR marriage.

HopeAtLast.com

Like What You've Read?

Check what is Also Available

on EncouragingBookstore.com & Amazon.com

Scan the code below to the available books for our Abundant Life, Restored and By the Word of Their Testimony series.

Please visit our Websites where you'll also find these books as FREE Courses for both men and women.

Want to know more how you can Live an Abundant Life?

Restore Ministries International

POB 830 Ozark, MO 65721 USA
For more help
Please visit one of our Websites:

EncouragingWomen.org

HopeAtLast.com

LoveAtLast.org

RestoreMinistries.net

Aidemaritale.com (French)

AjudaMatrimonial.com (Portuguese)

AmoreSenzaFine.com (Italian)

AyudaMatrimonial.com (Spanish)

Eeuwigdurendeliefde-nl.com (Dutch)

EvliliginiKurtar.com (Turkish)

EternalLove-jp.com (Japanese)

Pag-asa.org (Filipino)

Uiteindelikhoop.com (Afrikaans)

Zachranamanzelstva.com (Slovak)

Wiecznamilosc.com (Polish)

EncouragingMen.org